Family Matters *Why Homeschooling Makes Sense*

Family Matters *Why Homeschooling Makes Sense*

David Guterson

A Harvest Book
Harcourt Brace & Company
San Diego   New York   London

Requests for permission to make copies of any part
of the work should be mailed to the following
address: Permissions Department, Harcourt, Inc.,
6277 Sea Harbor Drive, Orlando, Florida 32887-6777.

Portions of this book previously appeared in different
form in *Harper's Magazine*.

Library of Congress Cataloging-in-Publication Data
Guterson, David.
Family matters: why homeschooling makes sense/David Guterson.
—1st Harvest ed.
p. cm.—(Harvest book)
Includes bibliographical references and index.
ISBN 0-15-630000-1
1. Homeschooling—United States. I. Title.
LC40.G89   1993
649'.68—dc20   93-5042

Designed by Lori McThomas
Printed in the United States of America
First Harvest edition 1993
M L K J I H G F E D

Acknowledgments

My thanks to Brian Ray, Jon Wartes, and Sandi Hall for generously sharing sources and research. I am also greatly indebted to Patrick Farenga for taking an interest in this book from the beginning and for his invaluable suggestions and insights.

Many public educators were kind to me and provided assistance and information, among them Betsy Abrams and Carol Nimick of the Twin Ridges School District, Eleanor Hill of the Lake Washington District, and Marci Van Cleave and Marcia Harris in Chimacum, Washington.

Colin Harrison provided early encouragement and deft editorial advice; he gracefully urged me to think clearly in print about educational matters. Anne Borchardt prompted me to focus on education at a time when my attention was wandering, and Leigh Haber's enthusiasm for the book did much to keep me at it. Alane Salierno Mason stayed with me the whole way—her devotion to the manuscript is discernible on every one of its pages.

I am grateful to many friends, colleagues, and neighbors for reading various parts of the book and for taking the time to comment on it: Julia Wan, Marilyn Place, Phil McCrudden, Matt Johnson, Barbara Chrisman, Ralph and Deborah Cheadle. My father, Murray Guterson, also read and discussed parts of the book with me and assisted in my research into legal matters. Alan and Lois Park, Larry and Jill Miller, and Bob and Ann Radwick have all been extremely generous to me in a variety of ways. Their kindness is much appreciated.

My children—Taylor, Travis, and Henry—asked the kinds of questions about what I was doing that encouraged me to do it better. I am grateful to them for their curiosity and goodwill and for their conversation.

Finally, I am deeply grateful to Robin Radwick Guterson for her close reading, incisive commentary, and love.

Contents

Family Matters *Why Homeschooling Makes Sense*

Introduction

To the oft-cited triumvirate of what is ineluctable in life—birth, death, and taxes—we Americans are prone to add an unspoken fourth: school.

In fact, we Americans share an allegiance to school that remains for the most part unarticulated. Many of us see schools as the foundation of our meritocracy and the prime prerequisite to a satisfying existence. School is the institution sine qua non, the elemental experience of childhood. Most of us cannot imagine an American youth today without hallways, classrooms, and cafeteria trays; the kind of locker flirtations immortalized in cinema; homework, varsity basketball games, chalkboards, and multiple-choice examinations. School is so deeply ingrained in us that a call for learning outside of it, without it, can sound as strange as a call for us to try to live without food. School is inevitable; school is a fact of life.

In my classroom at a high school in an upper-middle-class milieu where education is taken, in relative terms, seriously, we read with great purpose precisely those stories that tacitly reaffirm this loyalty to schools: In *Lord of the Flies* a pack of schoolboys degenerate into killers because no teachers are around to preserve the constraints of civilization; in *To Kill a Mockingbird* the venerable Atticus insists that, for all its shortcomings—and despite the fact that Scout is best educated by his own good example and by life in the larger web of Maycomb County (and that Atticus himself never went to school)—Maycomb Elementary is mandatory. *Catcher in the Rye* is in large part the story of its protagonist's maladjustment to schools, and though J. D. Salinger is highly critical of the hypocrisy behind a "good education" he ultimately offers up Mr. Antolini—an English teacher—as Holden Caulfield's last best hope. Finally, *A Separate Peace* might explicitly condemn the neurotic competitiveness of school life, but its implicit message—the one that gets taught in schools, anyway—is that Gene Forrester should have paid closer attention to his English teachers while they discoursed on the nature of evil.

The doctrine of school's necessity, which we early imbibe in the very belly of the beast, is inevitably supplemented once we're disgorged. The daily implacability with which the media report the decline of schools, the constant knell of ominous statistics on the sorry state of American education, the curious popularity of such books as E. D. Hirsch, Jr.'s *Cultural Literacy* and Allan Bloom's *The Closing of the American Mind*—these are portents, foremost, but they also serve to reinforce our shared assumption that school is required not merely because we attended it but also because our common life is so precarious. Our national discussion about education is a desperate one, taking place, as it does, in an atmosphere of crisis, but it does not include in any serious way a challenge to the notion that every child should attend school. Why? Because, quite simply, there is no context for such a challenge; because we live in a country where a challenge to the universal necessity of schools is considered not merely eccentric, not merely radical, but fundamentally un-American.

Furthermore, we Americans are likely to view schools as the supreme agents of democracy and—as E. D. Hirsch would have it—of cultural literacy. Jefferson's vision, after all, was that school would function as democracy's proving ground, a place where all comers would take their best shot at the American dream and where that dream would ultimately find its most

basic and enduring sustenance. Not to show up at all—at all!
—is thus to give in to the forces of cultural decline, to withdraw
at the moment of national crisis, and to suggest openly that if
Rome is really burning, the best response is not to douse the
flames or even to fiddle away beside the baths but to go home
and lock the door.

Our schools are celebrated daily in public-service advertisements (on MTV, for example, which exhorts students to stay
in school in order to make something of themselves, and at time-
outs during NBA basketball games) as conduits of upward mo-
bility for the poor and disenfranchised; they are, at least in our
history books, the best opportunity for the children of immigrants to gain a purchase on the American dream. Schools have
gradually become associated in our minds with what is finest
about our political and economic traditions. Our democratic
sentiments, it turns out—so deeply felt, so altogether vital to
our national identity—prevent us, ironically, from seeing the
democratic possibilities of a society in which many children
learn outside of government-operated institutions.

Many of us view schools as the primary training ground for
the social life we experience when at last we emerge from them:
In halls and classrooms, we recollect with mixed emotions, we
sorted out the broad panoply of human types, or the vast spectrum of American personalities, anyway, and then adjusted ourselves to them, found ways to modulate our own personas in
the face of the great shifting tide of American humanity. As
adults we believe that our understanding of others was developed first and foremost on school playgrounds and in classrooms; we feel that those without the experience of school are
condemned to remain eternal outsiders, aliens who will live
forever uninitiated into the tricky nuances of adult society. They
will miss their cues at cocktail parties, for example; they will

not understand the subtleties of behavior that come their way at the office or on the bus. The necessity of jocularity at the proper moment—or of self-effacement or bluster or silence or roaring laughter—will be entirely lost on these extraterrestrials, and when they meet someone essential at a sales conference they will be unable to place him on the list of types they knew at school. They will be, in this view, like caterpillars who never become butterflies, crawling along down the labyrinths of adult life and blinking unhappily at the shrubbery.

Then, too, many of us are entrenched believers in the absolute necessity of the school of hard knocks and in the notion that our finest virtues as adults are the result of school's hardships. We remember quite vividly that we suffered in school, in large and small ways, at the hands of our teachers, at the hands of our peers, and we tend to feel, in retrospect, that these sufferings were formative experiences of the sort that steeled us for the myriad sufferings of adult life. School was the place where we had to struggle for our cookie, where some bigger boy shoved us from our place in line or stole our blocks or vandalized our finger paintings, where we learned forbearance and self-reliance and met in the form of our teachers adults who were less than perfect, less than fully attentive to our every need—where, in short, life in all its troubling glory presented itself to us daily. A dark inversion, perversely true, of Robert Fulghum's *Everything I Need to Know I Learned in Kindergarten*.

It turns out that our memories of school, shot through with nostalgia, prevent us from thinking objectively about it. Having attended ourselves, having experienced it as part and parcel of our childhoods, we have become believers in its necessity. School as we know it—an invention of the last century and a half, I should point out—is today a cultural assumption so pervasive that ultimately we do not recognize it as such: Like birth, death,

4

and taxes it is simply *there*, much discussed perhaps, but unavoidable.

Pinned down by the forces of ideology and culture, by social consensus and our common mythologies, we have thus far in America been unable to treat fairly the notion that not every child need necessarily attend school, that many might indeed flourish beautifully outside of it, and that our society might actually derive significant benefits by promoting and nurturing what we have come to call *homeschooling*, a term that is in essence a powerful misnomer, a newspeak word for the attempt to gain an education outside of institutions. A *homeschooler* is not really a *home*schooler at all but rather a young person who does not go to school, a person best defined by what he does not do as opposed to by what he does. (It is sometimes used, too, to describe his parents, so that the term has often a double meaning: It encompasses both children who do not go to school and those who guide them in school's stead.) There are currently upward of 300,000 homeschoolers in America—truants from one perspective, perhaps, but following in the footsteps, too, of George Washington, Abraham Lincoln, Woodrow Wilson, Theodore Roosevelt, Thomas Edison, Frederick Douglass, Margaret Mead, Andrew Carnegie, Mark Twain, Charlie Chaplin, Andrew Wyeth, Pearl Buck, George Washington Carver, and Albert Einstein.

It is no coincidence that currently a substantial majority of homeschooling parents in America are fervently religious and that most of the rest might best be characterized as the philosophical heirs of Jean-Jacques Rousseau. The former view the schools as at odds with Christian doctrine, the latter as at odds with Man the Individual. Starting from these distinctly separate premises they have nevertheless arrived at the common conviction that they do not want their children in schools.

The homeschooling movement is also polarized by a general disagreement regarding educational methods. At one extreme are the orthodox "structuralists" whose homes are essentially miniature schools with formal and conventional curricula. At the other are advocates of "unstructured learning" (among them quibblers about the semantic inaccuracy of the *structured-unstructured* dichotomy) whose guiding principle is trust in the child's innate ability to learn even if parents do *no* formal teaching. In between the vast majority spreads itself along a spectrum that includes nearly everything.

Homeschooling parents may be a diverse lot—the conservative and the progressive, the fundamentalist Christian and the libertarian, the urban, the rural, the idealist, the social skeptic, the self-sufficient and the paranoid—yet studies of them show little or no relationship between the degree of religious content in a homeschooling program or the level of its formal structure or the education or affluence of homeschooling parents and the surprising academic success of homeschooled children, who tend to score well above the norm on standardized achievement tests.

Despite this—and despite the fact that teaching one's own was pervasive in America until the mid-nineteenth century—homeschooling today is little more than a fringe movement, an uprising perceived by many as a sort of insult and by others as a severe admonishment: "Take more interest in your children, like us!" homeschooling parents appear to be saying. The movement, in short, has a public-relations problem. It inspires the sort of unease normally reserved for the isolate, the heretic, or the cultist.

Public disapproval of the homeschooling movement has another dimension perhaps best characterized as simultaneously religious and political. Many homeschooling families are fervently Christian, many of them outraged by the secular nature of our national life, many compelled to homeschool not from purely educational notions but primarily from religious convictions. Some see homeschooling as a brand of political resistance to an essentially secular and relativistic society; others feel certain God Himself has ordained that they must homeschool. They will quote from Scripture words to the effect that God expects parents to educate their own, that God does not *permit* parents to delegate that responsibility, particularly not to the public schools—"places," as one writer tells us in *The Christian Educator*, "where a carefully maintained atmosphere of materialism, humanism, evolution, relativism, and sometimes downright atheism is deliberately created for the impressionable student." For fundamentalist Christians homeschooling is a political statement as much as an educational strategy, and because of this they are both vigorous and prominent in the national homeschooling movement. Thus the public, when it thinks of homeschooling, thinks of fundamentalists first and foremost and has come to loosely associate homeschooling with Christian talk shows and conservative politics. Throw in, for good measure, a few harmless and wide-eyed granola heads, romantic libertarians, and idealistic progressives, and you've got the whole bizarre recipe.

Few people realize that the homeschooling movement also includes many professional educators—parents who teach in the public schools but keep their children outside of them. Their paradoxical behavior makes them at times a curiosity and at times an affront to the schools that hire them; their students are confounded by their apparent hypocrisy; their colleagues are apt to tread lightly around the subject if they enter its terrain at all. So saying I'll add this personal confession: I am one of these walking contradictions. I teach my neighbors' children in my high-school classroom, but my wife and I teach ours at home.

We came to it, I should admit from the outset, viscerally, with our understanding incomplete, pondering no more than a year's trial run. We were like most parents in the turmoil we felt far in advance of our first child's first step onto the school bus, but we were unlike most in our response to it: We became existentially worried.

At first it seemed this anxiety must signify something fundamentally wrong with us. Were we overzealous, overprotective, paranoid? Were we like Allie Fox in Paul Theroux's *The Mosquito Coast*, psychotically certain that society is irredeemable and destroying our children to protect them from it? It was our duty, we tried to tell ourselves, to override our parental instincts: School, after all, was ineluctable. So my wife attempted to visit the local kindergarten (to no avail—its principal's policy forbade such visits) in order to assure herself that nothing dreadful might occur within its walls. Meanwhile I sought to convince myself that my own experience of student life as nightmarishly dreary and an incomparable waste of time was my own experience, nothing more, and that nothing legitimate could be deduced from it. This was true: I could deduce nothing.

I wish I could write that my wife and I had excellent reasons for deciding to homeschool. We didn't, however. It was not a matter of compelling logic (although sound reasons have kept us at it since then). It was in the gut, and the gut, we knew, could be wrong. In May of that year—six years ago now—we contemplated books on education; in June we talked, July we wrung hands, August felt deep and hot and still, September came, and then one morning the big yellow school bus arrived, waited for a moment with its doors swung open, and our child did not get on it.

That fall we took to answering our inquisitors—friends, acquaintances, siblings, grandparents—with the all-purpose and ultimately evasive assertion that to hold a child out of kindergarten was not really so unusual, that many people, all kinds, do it.

"Not schoolteachers," they replied.

Since then each of our three sons has missed the bus, so to speak, and we have gradually discovered that there are excellent reasons for sustaining this state of affairs.

With one foot firmly in each educational camp—a public-school teacher and a homeschooling parent—I set out to write a book about families and education. I have tried to keep in mind the seriousness of asking parents to reassess their commitment to schools at a time when many voices in education are calling for a greater commitment to them. I have not encouraged parents to withdraw their children from schools, nor have I meant to offer homeschooling as a panacea for our nation's educational ills. Finally, I do not claim any sort of moral superiority for homeschooling parents nor do I hold them up as exemplary. My central notion has been a simple one: that parents are critical to education and therefore public educators—and everyone else—can learn much from those who teach their own.

Like all people homeschooling parents make mistakes, fall short in various ways, act on faulty premises—in sum are prone to the whole gamut of educational folly and failure. But they have also wrought some astonishing successes, and these warrant our examination. I have tried to make a case for the academic, social, and political efficacy of homeschooling (Chapters 1–4) and to offer a number of useful perspectives from which homeschooling might be viewed (Chapters 5–9). I have also suggested some ideas for cooperation between school districts and homeschooling families (Chapter 10) and have concluded by describing some of the fulfillments in store for parents who choose to educate their children. My approaches to these matters have been intentionally various—narrative, anecdote, personal experience, analysis, reflection, comparison, contrast—in the hope of sustaining my reader's interest.

My deeper hope, though, is that family-centered education will someday gain legitimacy and will eventually be incorporated into our national system of education. I also hope that the term *homeschooling* will fade with time as Americans come to recognize that every home, every community, is a place in which education should go forward—and where they in fact cause it to go forward with the assistance and support of school systems.

Finally, while I might already have described myself as a walking contradiction—a homeschooling parent and a public educator—I see no real conflict in what I am doing and remain committed to both worlds. At school I come to admire many of my students, to like them so well that I am sad to see them go; at school there are moments in which I am gratified, even moved, by a sentence a student has written in an essay, by a question somebody asks. Yet for all this, for all the quiet joys of the classroom, I am forever aware of some amorphous dissatisfaction, some inkling that things might be better. It seems to me that many of my students should simply be elsewhere, that they would be better served by a different sort of education, that their society would be better served by it too. I believe this education is one their parents can help provide and that their parents should expect schools to assist them in providing it, should help create a community that nurtures learning. They love their children with a depth I can't match, finally; and finally teaching is an act of love before it is anything else.

1

Teacher, Parent

We schoolteachers constantly complain—into a steady, implacable wind—that with much smaller classes and more one-to-one contact we might make better academic headway. Small wonder, then, that homeschoolers score consistently well on standardized achievement tests: they're learning alone or in groups small enough to make real academic success possible.

But a strong case has been made recently that standardized achievement tests don't tell us very much that matters, first because they are culturally biased, and second because they are achievement *tests* and tests are attended by varied levels of anxiety and by a wide range of test-taking habits. Homeschoolers, it turns out, are predominantly from the middle class that standardized achievement tests purportedly favor, and their parents are for the most part strongly committed to their education as well as better educated themselves than the average American adult. (A 1986 study comparing private to homeschooled children yielded closely corresponding standardized test scores, though the mean income of homeschooling families is far lower—between $20,000 and $30,000 annually. One plausible interpretation is that the crucial factor in test success is not parental affluence but parental commitment to education.) We should also consider that some homeschooling parents teach "to" standardized tests—some classroom teachers do so as well—because states require that their children take them or because college entry is largely contingent on test scores in the absence of a school grade point average. This coaching, of course, can greatly influence scores: The Educational Testing Service advises that forty-five hours of it will yield a thirty-point gain on the SAT, or Scholastic Aptitude Test.

So while I might be tempted to assert that learning out of schools is in some general way superior to learning in them, I don't much trust the standardized test results that on the surface bear this out. These tests, it appears, are inherently unsound measures of learning, in part because of factors I have described, in part because we have yet to formulate a satisfactory description of what learning is about, of what it is we seek to measure when we measure learning.

In fact, most of the measures schools have devised to determine educational success yield problematic results. The majority of public-school teachers know this so well that when asked to describe the difficulties of their task they will soon mention the dark travail of evaluation: essays, tests, quizzes, and assignments designed to measure the learning of young people but in reality measuring the approximate degree of their adjustment to life at school.

Take, for example, the ubiquitous unit test, that staple of teachers in American schools, which seeks to measure, presumably, both the quantity and quality of a student's learning during a given period of time. In my high-school English classes I have sometimes administered this style of exam: one on, say, Robert Frost; another on cummings, Jeffers, Stevens, and Sandburg; a third on Hemingway; a fourth on Fitzgerald. Many of my students have become sleekly expert at taking these, chiefly because they have come to understand the full set of assumptions inherent in them. They are content tests, my students know, designed to ferret out what they have gathered in the way of information about, among other things, Frost's use of rhyme scheme or Hemingway's use of understatement. The test will demand of them both adrenaline and mental focus, a careful balance of clarity and nervousness that should begin brewing the evening before during a controlled and methodical last study session culminating in plenty of sleep. It will demand they bring with them no hunger or restlessness, no personal anxieties or outside problems—or that they keep those things, with the test before them, out of mind. They should bring, too, a finely tuned comprehension of the art of school test taking: when and when not to raise their hands to request illumination or deciphering (taking into account the various kinds of embarrassment that might accrue from their peers), how far to push me in search of explanations or outright clues, in what order the questions might best be answered, how to organize their time, how best to reassess their chosen answers. The test, for them, should be the culmination of a strategy they have been busily employing since the unit on Frost began two weeks earlier: uncovering what it is I will demand of them and gathering themselves to meet it—worthy skills, perhaps, and certainly of value in contexts beyond the present one but nevertheless disassociated entirely from the purposes for which the test was conceived and designed.

Anecdotal evidence may be superfluous, the conclusions we draw from it irrelevant, but nevertheless I point to the results of an informal experiment I have conducted five times in a ten-year teaching career. In this experiment I give a test on Friday, an ordinary objective test (true-false, matching, fill-in-the-blank, multiple choice) preceded by a Thursday review session and a week full of reminders that this test is on Friday, don't forget to reread this or that, to study those notes, to review this hand-out, to get plenty of rest, to see me if there are questions; I am furthermore explicit all week long about both the form of the test and its subject matter. In short I prepare them to meet the test in the time-honored tradition of high-school teachers.

Friday evening I take their completed tests home. Over the weekend I grade them. On Monday, with no prior warning of any sort, I give them the same test and ask them to take it again. Monday evening I grade those, staple them to the Friday exam, and hand both back to students.

None—*no one*—has ever received an equal or higher grade on the test administered Monday. Most, in fact, receive a considerably lower grade, missing, often, twice as many questions on Monday as they missed on Friday.

My point is not that school children have poor memories but that most measures of academic success, from general knowledge standardized achievement tests to the unit tests administered so pervasively in schools, are of dubious value at best. Learning, it turns out, is a mysterious process, nearly impossible to "measure." It goes forward in singular fashion in the mind of each individual. It does not lend itself readily to examinations designed to reveal its progress. Nevertheless examinations are to date what we have—for better or worse—and believers in their efficacy should take the hard numbers about homeschoolers and their academic performance seriously. They tell us that homeschoolers as a group score well above public schoolers in all categories of the widely used Stanford Achievement Test except mathematical computation, where they are merely at the norm (though, interestingly, they score well above the norm in mathematical *applications*). In many categories they score in or above the sixtieth to seventieth percentile. In Oregon, Tennessee, Pennsylvania, Montana,

Washington, Alaska, and elsewhere the results are uniformly good, and the evidence continues to pile up—so much of it that the educational establishment in this country, which relies so heavily on standardized tests as measures of academic success or failure, must sooner or later come to terms with the fact that by its own definition homeschooling is an astonishing success.

Perhaps more astonishing is that despite a disadvantage inherent in their situation—they have no transcripts to present to admissions boards—homeschoolers are both enrolling and flourishing in our most prestigious colleges and universities. Harvard, Yale, Princeton, and many other schools have welcomed homeschoolers onto their campuses, and homeschoolers have left such places with high honors and prestigious scholarships. Grant Colfax, for example, left Harvard with a Fulbright to study livestock in New Zealand. Alexandra Swann began at Brigham Young at age twelve, finished her program at fourteen, then began work on a master's degree from California State University. It is, of course, still too early to tell what sorts of contributions these young people will make as adults; suffice it to say that past homeschoolers—Edison, Wyeth, Mead, Chaplin, Twain, and others—have made extraordinary contributions.

Both college success and high test scores have been achieved by homeschoolers from widely different backgrounds. It does not seem to matter, for example, how well educated homeschooling parents are or how wealthy or religious they are or if they are certified as professional educators or if the curriculum they devise for their children is highly structured or informal, time-consuming or swiftly finished. It does not seem to matter how old their children are or what sex they are or if they have been to school before or if they are new or experienced homeschoolers. Despite wide variation in all these things, which would seem on the surface to influence scores, homeschooled children from broadly varying backgrounds remain very similar in one regard: They do extraordinarily well on standardized achievement tests. The most important variable, it turns out— one that unites the entire group and one, I think, we can justly infer—is that all homeschoolers come from families devoted to the education of their young.

It seems to me, on the other hand, that we need no test scores to tell us this. Most of us recognize instinctively that parental commitment to education is easily the most essential factor in academic performance, and most of us would acknowledge that homeschooling parents, as a group, have this commitment by definition. It is worth noting that many political conservatives, those most likely to feel skeptical about homeschooling, are just as likely to articulate forcefully this connection between family and learning. William J. Bennett, secretary of education during the Reagan years, is emblematic of these voices. "All parents are teachers," he writes in *Our Children and Our Country*, "the all but indispensable teachers. And as teachers, parents always have had the first and largest responsibility for educating their children. . . . *The fact that we have established public schools is not a surrender by parents of their basic responsibility for education. Each parent still has that responsibility* [italics mine]."

Bennett is joined by Allan Bloom, whose 1987 *The Closing of the American Mind* mentions just about everything *except* homeschooling and yet simultaneously bemoans the fact that "hardly any homes have any intellectual life whatsoever, let alone one that informs the vital interests of life," that today's parents "lack self-confidence as educators of their children," and that today's children are "raised, not educated." E. D. Hirsch, author of the equally popular *Cultural Literacy: What*

Every American Needs to Know, also recognizes the connection between family and learning, suggesting in his discussion of family background and academic achievement "that the significant part of our children's education has been going on outside rather than inside the schools." Like Bennett and Bloom, Hirsch does not mention homeschooling; instead he argues that by changing the curricula of schools we can ensure that the significant part of our children's education will one day occur within their walls.

Hirsch's *Cultural Literacy*, which promotes a national curriculum, also dismisses the widely held view that family life is so significant to academic success that schools, no matter how arranged, cannot do much to equalize matters for children from educationally deprived backgrounds. Hirsch is of the opinion that changes in school curricula can negate or overcome differences in the family lives of children and lays partial blame for our "fatalistic conception" of schools on the well-known Coleman Report of 1966, which concluded that differences in academic success more strongly correlated with students' family background than with differences in the schools they attended.

Hirsch might dispute the findings of the Coleman Report, but he does not underestimate their impact. The Coleman Report touched off a national debate about how schools might cope with the academic differences between students from homes where education is promoted and homes where it is less so. It has been, perhaps, the single most influential piece of educational research done in America in the past thirty years, and its conclusions have been widely accepted. Curiously, however, few of our educational experts, in responding to it, have focused their attention on families or on how to nurture academic success in the homes of *all* Americans. Instead they offer endless new curricula and novel ways of organizing schools on the assumption that by so doing they will somehow negate the truth of the Coleman Report—that education begins at home.

Furthermore, most parents recognize that their own influence is critical to their children's learning. More than half of those polled recently by *Newsweek* said the role they play in their children's education is "extremely important," while just more than a third could say the same of schools and teachers. Meanwhile, Yale's James Comer has tested the notion that direct parental involvement in education might make a critical difference. Comer brought together teachers, administrators, receptionists, and parents at two New Haven elementary schools with reputations for poor academic performance, investing all in a joint-decision-making process that ultimately changed not only the life of classrooms but the commitment of families to education. As a result, says Comer, student achievement at both schools now ranks at or near the top when compared to other New Haven elementaries.

Consider, for a moment, education in Japan. We Americans are prone to regard Japan as the home of a rigid and merciless educational system that destroys individuality and produces automatons. We like to point to the suicide rate among its adolescents and denigrate its system of examinations. (Actually, the United States has led Japan since 1980 in its rate of adolescent suicides; furthermore, no consistent relationship exists between Japanese suicides and *shiken jigoku*, or "examination hell.") We might rightly refuse to learn from Japan on a number of counts, but we ought to keep in mind that Japanese schools work and work very well. Why? Chiefly because parents there have not yet taught themselves to leave education to the schools (nor have teachers, who are expected to spend time with the families of their students and to take it upon themselves to grasp the family context out of which the child comes). School administrators in Riverside, New York—home to a sizable Japanese population—were mystified recently to find many Japanese families purchasing two sets of textbooks for their children. They discovered, as Merry White recounts in *The Japanese Educational Challenge*, "that one set was for the mother, who would study one or more lessons ahead of her child to help him or her in schoolwork. The result was that Japanese children who entered school in September knowing little or no English often finished in June at the top of the class in all subjects."

In the end no argument or evidence is really needed to convince Americans of what they already know: Parents are crucial to the education of children, and family life is fundamental to academic success. These things are so obvious as to go without saying; the surprising thing is that in the face of them few of our foremost thinkers on education have yet listened to what homeschoolers have to tell us.

Homeschooling families differ vastly from one another not only in their choices about educational methods and content but also about the relationship of one to the other. The purchaser of a mass-market educational program providing fixed curricula, textbooks, work sheets, home video instruction, and the option to send a child's work to company headquarters for professional assessment and review (and when the curriculum is completed, transcripts and diplomas) might refuse for sound educational reasons to impose on a child a fixed and structured day of learning. Conversely, a true believer in *child-centered* learning—or *organic* learning or *holistic* learning—might nevertheless, and with a sense that so doing is utterly consistent, demand that a child spend two hours every weekday, from 7:00 A.M. to 9:00 A.M., at the kitchen table working on mathematics assignments. In other words, rigidity (or flexibility) regarding content does not necessarily imply the same regarding method —and vice versa, too.

A central truth lies behind all this, one that ought to be self-evident: namely, that many homeschooling families, when it comes to selecting and integrating methods and content, view the needs of their children, their particular learning styles and areas of interest, as the elemental consideration. Most do so instinctively, without any grounding in the educational research (volumes of it, incidentally, some touched on in Chapter Nine of this book), which emphatically confirms that such individualization of learning is an extremely good idea. As I have said already, standardized-test results show no relationship between the level of formal structure in a homeschooling program and homeschoolers' scores. If we choose to take this data seriously, it suggests that method and content in the abstract sense are not relevant to academic success but that discovering what methods and contents are right for individual children makes a profound difference.

We all know that each child differs from the next and that their academic needs are best met when we take these differences seriously. We also know that schools have enormous difficulties in this regard and are openly desperate to do better. Two pillars of the current educational debate—tracking of students and class size—are intimately connected to this larger question of individualizing education. Yet the novel approaches and creative solutions thus far conjured by educators have not altered the primary design flaw of schools: They are mass institutions and thus by definition ill suited to the academic needs of individuals.

Homeschooling parents have a distinct advantage over public-school teachers when it comes to individualizing education. Teachers at Bainbridge High School, where I am employed, generally meet with between 125 and 150 students daily—close to the national average for secondary-school teachers. Most are astonishingly good at uncovering the unique inner mechanics of at least some of these children, but most would readily admit, too, that even after ten weeks of class most students remain in essence strangers, somebody else's children, their private histories and intellectual idiosyncrasies mostly lost on them. We teachers must do the best we can to guess what it is each child needs and to make these guesses on the basis of limited experience and knowledge of each. (Tracy Kidder's Mrs. Zajac, the heroine of *Among Schoolchildren*, is an icon when it comes to this sort of guessing.) A large measure of the respect I hold for my colleagues derives from the efforts I see them make to get to know their students, yeomanly efforts to succeed against overwhelming odds and in the face of difficulties intrinsic to our job. Despite everything, many seek relentlessly to understand these scores of young people placed in our charge and to comprehend them as individuals. But even when we succeed, when we appear to ourselves to have guessed right about, say, how a child learns best, what methods and approaches work effectively with him or her, we find ourselves unable to do very much that is useful with this knowledge. Again, the mass nature of public education lies behind this failure on the part of teachers, and even the most committed and energetic are finally beaten down by it, so that a good year, a good day, is one in which only small gains are made in the face of any number of large defeats. For though we might come to know some small percentage of our students with some even smaller measure of sophistication, we are prevented by our duty to the vast majority from acting meaningfully on this knowledge. To quote teachers in a general fashion with a comment heard in faculty rooms everywhere: *There isn't enough time in the day.*

The purveyors of programs for individualizing instruction

in the face of massive numbers of students aren't coming to grips with reality. We can't get to know the large majority of our students, their inner lives, their personal histories, the workings of their minds, their social mechanics, with anything approaching the intimacy of parents, and we can't act very usefully on the limited knowledge of them we do acquire. For fewer than half the days of a single year—180 one-hour sessions at most public high schools—we see their faces among a crowd of faces; then they are gone forever. We are quite simply, and despite all our professional training in university schools of education, in a poor position to teach.

Homeschooling parents, on the other hand, find themselves uniquely well positioned to nurture learning in the lives of children. From the moment of their child's birth they have been immersed in an evolving and intimate relationship that allows them to shape educational experiences appropriate to that child. For them it is the nature of the child that defines both content and method, and it is the response of the child to content and method that suggests to them their future choices, new alternatives, other strategies. Curricula can be supplemented, revved up, altered, intensified, or momentarily abandoned; methods can be used in combination, in sequence or simultaneously, then revised as the child grows and changes month to month, even day to day. Uninhibited by the inherent inertia of schools—their uniformity of content and pedagogy—and intimately connected to their child's educational needs, homeschooling parents are able to invent and reinvent, learn from error, modulate as their understanding deepens, and finally nurture their child's intellectual growth from the advantageous position of one who loves that child deeply. In short, parents are natural teachers, positioned by the very structure of life to tend to the learning of their children.

As a public-school teacher and a homeschooling parent, I find myself moving between two worlds almost on a daily basis. School is the world of the fixed curriculum, an inert body of knowledge and skills to be disseminated on a fixed schedule. Its content is ultimately in the hands of professionals who have acquainted themselves with state and district guidelines and who exert themselves to stay in touch with the needs of the nation and community. They must also take into account the immense complications of large-scale schooling and adapt both curricula and methods to it so that the content of education can in fact be transmitted, or at least partially transmitted, against the odds. Thus the schedule of the day and year is made routine, because no other timetable of learning lends itself to an institution of such unwieldy proportions, and content is tailored to a sense of what the group needs rather than the individual. Creativity is limited by the sheer size of the student population and by the individual teacher's resolute commitment to meet the needs of the many, to commit to one method that has limited effectiveness but is at the same time the least of many evils. School is about "delivering instruction," "learner outcomes," "mastery of content," and "feedback with correction." It is in many ways an abstraction and a weariness to the spirit. Children, in the majority of cases, adapt to it against their wills.

Proponents of the school-of-hard-knocks approach will reply that this process of reluctant adaptation is a fine and necessary part of education and teaches young people the truth about adult life. *Expect to be misunderstood; expect to be bored by much of what comes your way; expect to be ignored, to have your needs go unmet, to have to adjust to the world—don't expect it to adjust to you.* They are right, of course, that these lessons must be learned and that schools teach these lessons exceedingly well, with great power, perhaps indelibly. The sad part is that in the process schools have also been exceedingly good at snuffing out the desire of many young people to understand their world. Schools have taught them to associate learning with this painful form of misunderstanding and with a frustrated boredom that ought to be the exception in their educational experience, not the rule. To acclimate students to misery under the rubric that so doing prepares them for life is a cynical notion—and a horrifying one. Rather, in shaping the academic experiences of our young we should recall that they are individuals who, with no help from our institutions—but because life simply is what it is—will learn by osmosis of the injustice of the adult world they will one day both define and inhabit.

Some schools have grudgingly and painfully come to terms with themselves but only in the face of mounting failures. Many now recognize that sooner or later they must confront the existence of individual learning styles and adapt to their reality. One response has been the adoption of "mastery-learning" programs, which break down a long series of educational objectives into incremental and sequential modest goals. Imagine a child seated alone, systematically making her way through a geography workbook, and you are imagining, in essence, mastery learning. Students master each humble step methodically, moving toward unit tests that are corrected and returned to them as "feedback." The idea here is to allow for a variety of learning rates without giving up the notion of a schoolwide curriculum. Students all continue to learn the same things; they simply learn them at rates better suited to their abilities.

Mastery learning has not been a panacea, though, chiefly because individual teachers are hugely overburdened by the daily task of administrating its details for such large numbers of students. (I have tried it myself. Thirty workbooks. Thirty students traveling at different rates through them, clamoring for attention when they stumble. Three are taking unit tests. Two are on page four of Book One, four are ripping through Book Three, five are bogged down in the middle of Book Two. I am trotting from the raised hand in row one to the raised hand in row four when the bell suddenly rings.) Mastery learning has, too, a pair of fatally flawed premises: that children learn best when the world is deconstructed into endless small components, and that method is ascendant over content (so the uniform subject matter of the workbooks is never called into question). Teachers who commit themselves to the concept and employ it in their classroom see very little transference of learning from the system's workbooks and progressive tests to the student's larger frame of reference. They find, ironically, that what their students have in fact "mastered"—if they master anything—is not some desired set of knowledge and skills but rather the mastery-learning system itself and the strategies required to confront it: reading between the lines of a workbook, for example, or filling in blanks with force-fed terms or ruling out deceptive multiple-choice options on a series of predictable examinations.

Progressive homeschoolers are apt to see mastery learning as a marked improvement over the strategies that preceded it but still not very useful. Many are dedicated to the proposition that real learning takes place in the world beyond institutions and that no "instructional delivery system" can begin to approach the instruction delivered by life itself. They see the content of education—the knowledge and skills an education develops—as emerging out of experience in the world and not out of classrooms and workbooks. Grounded by reading or inclination in the educational theories of Jean-Jacques Rousseau—who believed that young people develop best when adults refrain from imposing on them—these homeschoolers seek an education for their children free from coercion and control. "What children need," wrote the late John Holt, a leading voice among progressive homeschoolers, "is not new and better curricula but *access* to more and more of the real world; plenty of time and space to think over their experiences, and to use fantasy and play to make meaning out of them; and advice, road maps, guidebooks, to make it easier for them to get where they want to go (not where we think they ought to go), and to find out what they want to find out."

But rigid or flexible, progressive or traditional, true education always begins with the child and with an understanding of her individual needs. Whether one puts before her a fixed curriculum or a mastery-learning program or nurtures "access to more and more of the real world" is a function of the child's unique requirements as a learner. No curriculum or method is "best," and no philosophical premise about education supreme or universally applicable. Endless diversity is called for in the face of the endless diversity of children. Our methods and curricula ought to be implied by who they are and by what they individually need.

This diversity cannot be adequately addressed by schools as they currently operate, nor can it be addressed by homeschooling parents so thoroughly entrenched in their philosophical notions that their theory obscures the needs of their children. Abstractions about what works universally in education are best made secondary to the real needs of each child, while knowledge about what nurtures each should be acted on by those in a position to do so ably—whether they be teachers or parents or both together. The principle I suggest has a name among educators: *child-centered education*. It has come to mean a lot of things, but the term ought principally to remind us of our duty to shape the how and what of education not around a kernel of philosophical abstraction but around the needs of each unique child.

So while we might agree with Hirsch and others that there is a set of things all Americans need to know in order to be culturally literate (if not about what goes in that set), we should also resist the notion of a universal method to arrive there and insist that this literacy not be achieved at the expense of each child's love of learning. A belief in the importance of cultural literacy, in other words, should not prevent us from taking child-centered education seriously, for *child-centered* does not imply that each child simply go his own way in pursuit of a self-absorbed curriculum. It does imply, on the other hand, that children in particular and families in general should exercise primary control over content, and it also implies a general faith in the far-reaching curiosity and inquisitiveness of young people. While such faith may not come easily to Hirsch and other proponents of a national curriculum, it in fact paves the way for children to grasp important matters with a depth and breadth far superior to the *Dictionary of Cultural Literacy*. Placing the child at the center of his education does not put our culture, by extension, on the periphery; on the contrary, it lays the groundwork for successfully bringing the two together, for instilling in him a lifelong thirst for understanding his world.

Child-centered education puts into perspective, too, the debate about when children should start learning. Progressive homeschoolers characterize this debate as irrelevant: Children, they point out, are learning all the time, are learning even as they grow in the womb, thus the question about "beginning" at four or six or eight is for them a meaningless one. Opposite them stand advocates of intensive preschooling who espouse formal academic training for toddlers and even conscious attempts on the part of parents to educate their infants. Researchers, meanwhile, have made massive efforts to determine the proper age for initiating education and have come up with a variety of answers. Ultimately, burdened by the weight of endless administrative considerations, our schools go on operating under the assumption that at age six—the first grade—the formal education of all American children should begin.

The child-centered response to this is obvious. Homeschoolers need not concern themselves with the one best age to begin an education—as researchers have and as schools must—but rather with the needs and interests of the individual child. We begin when they are ready—neither before nor after. This demands an intimate awareness on our part, an awareness that comes quite naturally to parents but to almost nobody else.

Educators in the past ten years have become increasingly fond of the term *child-centered* in discussing school reform. What many have failed to recognize is that the public-school teacher is in no position to place most children at or even near the center of their own learning. Even the most committed teacher, overwhelmed by sheer numbers and by the structure of school itself, must fail to arrive at the profound understanding of each child that is a prerequisite to his or her success. It is parents who possess this profound understanding and who are well positioned to act on it.

Our own children—like children everywhere—made readily apparent when they were very young the nuances and idiosyncrasies of their learning styles and instructed us in the ways we might fail or succeed at the task of nurturing their educations. Each, of course, learns in a singular way, at a singular rate, and like every other child in the world instinctively and naturally pursues his education unless something or somebody prevents him.

Our family is fortunate to rent a home with a large and open yard behind it, a grassy expanse rimmed with alder trees where our boys can be found on sunny afternoons playing games with other children from the neighborhood. Our sons each learned to ride a bicycle here, and in so doing provided us with significant insight into who they are and how they pursue the acquisition of a desired skill.

Taylor, for example, our oldest boy, articulated for some time prior to an initial practice session an interest in riding a bicycle. He wanted to discuss it and to look at bicycles, but he did not want to get on one. He asked to see me ride and formulated questions about the brakes and pedals but remained hesitant about engaging the bike itself. Finally, after a lot of open and private soul-searching about the nature of bravery and fear and desire, Taylor, at age five, saddled up with the oft-repeated insistence that I not let go of the handlebars. So we went about like that, with me trotting along beside him while he held on feeling panicked and tight, and this went on through perhaps five sessions before he one day accepted that I might momentarily let go of the bike without jeopardizing his safety. The duration of my disengagements lengthened, the distance between myself and the boy on the bicycle grew greater. Taylor toppled over half a dozen times, discovering on each occasion that there was no great pain in it, that his fear was not commensurate with the potential injury at hand. He took great joy in this discovery—that in effect there was nothing to worry about—and as his anxiety dissolved his absorption in his bicycle grew into an obsession. He mastered its fine points shortly, with much happiness, but—as I have indicated—only after a lengthy, gentle, and cautious approach during which he'd pleaded openly for information and guidance.

Our middle son, Travis, grew up in a world where bicycle riding was a fact of life and where the risks it entailed had already been confronted by an older brother. It was clear to him, on a daily basis, as he went about his business in the yard, that a bicycle could in fact be mastered by somebody not too different from himself—a little older, perhaps, but not essentially different. At age three he picked up the bicycle where Taylor had left it and began the task of figuring out how to get onto the seat. Any suggestions from Robin and me as to how this might most effectively be accomplished were loudly spurned, and he quickly taught us to say nothing. Travis seemed motivated by a demonic frustration. He awoke on five successive mornings and went immediately to confront Taylor's bicycle. Yet what he knew to be possible and what he could actually *do* remained two separate things. We watched from across the yard while he battled the mysteries of bicycle riding, and if we tried to intervene in the process it was to no avail whatsoever. He wanted to be left alone with the object of his obsession and he let us know this fiercely.

So we stood by while he teetered down the yard's slope and rode headfirst into a volleyball standard. He cried for thirty seconds and rubbed his eyes, then climbed back onto the seat. When he was satisfied that what he was doing constituted *riding*, he pronounced himself a bicycle rider and urged everybody in the family to witness what he'd taught himself. It was true: He'd taught himself—and quickly. We hadn't even placed the bike in his path. He'd found it, and because he'd wanted to, he'd gone to work in his own inimitable manner.

Henry, our youngest, had *two* bike riders doing figure eights in his backyard, but for him this was a form of intimidation. When I asked him if he would like to learn too, he told me yes, he thought he would, but there was no eagerness in his voice. I brought out the bicycle and showed it to him, whereupon he informed me that he would learn to ride it when he was older, that he wasn't ready yet, that he didn't want to, he wasn't sure. We went through this ritual many times: Henry indicating an interest in bicycle riding, then backing away when the bicycle was before him, then assuring himself that the time would come when he was four, next year—*maybe*. Sure enough, when next year came, he began to ask both Robin and me to guide the bicycle along—gently—while he poked at the pedals and seized the handlebars between his fingers. There was a prolonged period in which we did this for Henry, letting go for split seconds now and then, moments about which he had mixed emotions. He wanted us there, hovering over him, and he wanted complete control over the process too. We could not let go of the bicycle until he said we could, though there was nothing really selfish in his plea, and a part of him wanted to be free of us. He wanted to learn, gravely, needed our help, and told us so. It was up to us to decide if we could adjust ourselves to his program and to discover in ourselves the required patience. We did (though it took us a while), and Henry gradually learned to ride, in the final stages on his own, with deliberateness of purpose and relief.

These stories, of course, are extended analogies, metaphors for each boy's style of learning—the sort of stories all parents have to tell. We have tried not to make too much of them or to apply them universally. My point is that the manner of each in learning to ride a bicycle is something we can place in a much larger context of understanding about our boys. The result is an education tuned to their harmonies—local and intimate as opposed to generic and imposed—an education that serves their inner worlds as well as the larger world they inhabit. Their education is alive, participatory, whole, and most of all *theirs*. It does not suggest to them that learning is separate from life, an activity that begins at a specific point in the morning and arbitrarily ends at another in the afternoon. Instead, learning proceeds from our children, out of their interests and questions. A winter day on which snow begins to fall is the natural starting point for discussion and reading about meteorology, weather fronts, road salts, sloped roofs, Alaska, polar bears, the invention of touring skis—each boy according to his interests. A spring evening spent on a blanket in the yard as the stars begin to show themselves is a proper time for talk of constellations with Taylor, bringing out a star chart Travis will look at, questions from Henry about satellites, setting up a telescope for all three boys, inquiries about eclipses, comets, meteors, navigation, Columbus, the Apollo space program. When the weather is poor for roaming out-of-doors, our sons—five, seven, and nine—might spend hours playing Scrabble or chess, or they might read to one another or draw pictures or comb through atlases and encyclopedias because the maps and pictures interest them. At dinner, if it is war in the Middle East that is in the news, the atlases and encyclopedias might end up on the table, and we might be there for two hours or more, eating, asking questions, looking up precise answers, discovering how it is that oil is formed in the ground, why it is that people fight over it, and how does Islam differ from other religions? and why does a person have to drink more water when it's hot? and why do camels have humps? At other times I'll hear them in another room discussing matters among themselves, elaborating on my explanations, illuminating for one another some point their mother has made, each in his own manner. Their interests, abilities, and vocabularies of course vary, but the intimacy they share on a daily basis provides common ground.

There are hours in the morning—two at most—when Robin sits down with our nine-year-old and is systematic about writing and mathematics; later they will practice their violins together. Evenings currently are my time for nurturing our children's interest in geography, for reading poems to them before they go to bed and for discussing the day's news. We are, or try to be, consistent about these matters, and yet no two days are ever much alike, and the curriculum, defined by our children, is devised by us according to their needs, implemented by us according to our strengths and weaknesses as parents and teachers:

August 30:   reading: *The Wooden Horse*
                        violin: *Witches' Dance*
                        writing: letter to Adam, final draft
                        science: gas cannon, carbon dioxide

September 26:   visit to chicken butchering plant
                        Point Defiance Zoo
                        violin practice
                        journal writing

October 16:   neighborhood recycling
                        banking
                        violin practice
                        Chess Club
                        finished letter to Aunt Mary

November 7:   *Mouse and the Motorcycle*, Chapters 3 and 4
                        math drill, multiplying by 4 and 5
                        violin practice
                        writing in cursive
                        swimming with Nathan

What else? An ant farm, a bug jar, a pair of field glasses, a rabbit cage, old appliances to take apart. An aquarium, a terrarium, a metronome, a collection of petrified wood and another

33

of shells, a globe, a magnifying glass, a calculator, a micro-scope. Felt pens, watercolors, magnets, dry-cell batteries, paper-airplane kits. Swimming teachers, Little League coaches, lithographers, bakers, canoe builders, attorneys, inventors, flutists, fishermen. And time to ponder all of them. To read the information on the backs of baseball cards, dig butter clams, dye rice paper, weave on a miniature table loom. To plant potatoes, tell tall tales, watch birds at the feeder. To fashion a self in silence.

And other people, many of them, a large and shifting variety. Friends from Little League and music lessons, acquaintances made at a nearby park, on the basketball court, in art classes, in the neighborhood, at a home for the elderly. The group of homeschoolers with whom they put on plays of their imagining, perform on piano, violin, and recorder, beachcomb at low tide, play chess. And visits to the Mack Gallery, the Grand Coulee Dam, the Ballard Locks, the Marine Science Center, the Museum of Flight. The Volunteer Park Conservatory and the Fishermen's Terminal. The Children's Theater and the State Capitol Build-ing, the Gingko State Park Petrified Forest. *The Miracle Worker*, a Makah storyteller, an Irish balladeer, a West African drum troupe, a marionette show, a sheep farm. A lithography studio, an inventor's workshop, a medieval fair. The Japanese-American community dinner, the Glugbin mask dance, the Frye Art Museum quilt exhibit.

And salmon. Perhaps it began one night with merely eating one. Or with reading *Red Tag Comes Back*. Or with the neigh-bor who fishes in Alaska for a living or the man at the side of the road with the purse seining net laid out in his yard. At any rate, the salmon-life-cycle exhibit at the Seattle Aquarium and walking among the gillnetting boats at Fishermen's Terminal. And cleaning debris from a salmon stream, standing in it one

Saturday. Feeding the salmon fry, weekly, at a nearby holding pond, and measuring their growth and development, graphing changes in water temperature and flow, examining eggs, weighing out feed. Visiting the hatchery on the Elwha River, the fish ladders at the Rocky Reach Dam, the Science Center display on the Nootka people—how they smoked salmon for the winter, how they netted and speared them. Then seeing their grandfather's catch from the Hakai Peninsula, the bones and organs, the digestive tracts of fish—the blood and murder—and debating the morality of eating what was once living and the relative ethics of sport fishing. Another morning watching while a neighbor cures salmon eggs for bait, measuring and weighing salmon, cooking salmon. Then one day, abruptly—perhaps it is just that a plane has flown overhead or that they have seen from the yard a crow fly—abruptly it is *flight* that interests them, the Wright Brothers, Charles Lindbergh, Amelia Earhart, drag and lift and thrust and wingspan, the Museum of Flight, the Boeing plant, pitch, yaw and roll . . .

Public school teachers, however well-intentioned, simply cannot match this. My students come into my life as a teacher, and I into theirs when they attend my class, for a few months, part of a year, an hour a day, and then we separate. I do not know how they learned to ride bicycles or much else about them. I am not in a position to understand them, no matter how I might try. Whatever success my students and I meet results from a fortunate coincidence: that what and how I teach is what they in fact, and at the moment, want and need from me. At times it works, and we are gratified; at others—the majority of the time, if we are honest—we go through the motions of our mutual failure: mine to understand them, theirs to adapt to the demands of school against their will and against their design as singular human beings.

Our privilege as parents is to understand our children with the thoroughness that true education requires, and our duty is to act on this understanding both wisely and energetically. Certainly not many parents will feel this means they must pull their children out of schools. On the other hand, the notion of parents as teachers is, in the broad sense, neither extreme nor outlandish, and whether or not we choose to send our children to schools is secondary to the commitment we make to involve ourselves meaningfully in their educations. Finally, homeschooling is only the extreme form of a life in which all parents should take part. All parents are potentially teachers of the sort their children need them to be.

2

What About Democracy?

Like a lot of teachers I do other work in order to ensure that ends meet. That is why on a night last October I went gillnetting for salmon with Bill McFadden—a man with much to say about homeschooling—on board his sternpicker, the *Silver Mist.*

"No kids," Bill had warned me by telephone. "Your kids drove me crazy last time. Too many questions about every little thing; couldn't concentrate on what I was doing."

"They fell asleep," I'd answered. "By midnight they were out. Before that they hosed down the deck, remember? You *liked* having them along."

"Just the same," Bill had repeated, "no kids this time."

Puget Sound gillnetting is a nocturnal industry: You're legal from 5:00 P.M., on the verge of dusk, until well after dawn, at 9:00 A.M. That means sixteen hours on the water, most of it passed in darkness with the net beneath the waves, the deck lights turned out, and the boat drifting on the tide. The work demands that you concentrate, especially when other boats are fishing to the south, ferry traffic is running steadily to the north, and you're picking your net and drifting toward another gillnetter not happy to see you in the neighborhood. But even with all this there is time for conversation, with radio squelch as background noise, the stars overhead, and the expanse of black water spreading out around the boat. A gill net stays down for two or three hours before it's time to pick the salmon from it, the stray kelp, dogfish, odd sticks, and seaweed. The thing to do is to stay awake, pay attention, and talk about whatever comes to mind.

For Bill McFadden, on this night, what had come to mind was homeschooling. He knew my children didn't go to school and had decided to take me to task about it in a good-humored, time-passing way. Bill, like a lot of gill-netters, is an independent thinker, an Ann Arbor MBA whose opinions don't follow any particular party line; his judgments about things are unpredictable. He reads voraciously in the off-season; there is always a weathered paperback jammed in his back pocket. This solitary night work is his chosen profession and he does it without flair but also without any wasted movement. At forty he is inexorably losing his hair yet retains the soft freckles that must have made him as a teenager look younger and more vulnerable than he was. Like most gill-netters Bill wears calf-high rubber boots— their buckles sliced off to make them streamlined—and rubberized bib overalls. He looks like somebody who has been fishing for a while: The fish stink and ceaselessly bobbing deck don't faze him. Bill is quietly impressive.

He is, he tells me, bothered by homeschooling; he says it frankly and without apologizing. He has two children of his own, he adds, and he's been thinking about their education. There's a lot Bill doesn't like about the local elementary, and he's been giving homeschooling a place in his thoughts. He and his wife, Lee, have been talking about it in a halfhearted, exploratory way. "Reading about education too," he says, adjusting the bill of his Hyster cap. "That's why I brought you fishing, really. Pick your brain while I pick fish."

I ask Bill what bothers him exactly about homeschooling. We're up on the flying bridge over the bow of the *Silver Mist*, our deck chairs turned toward the stern where the net is set— we're keeping our eyes on it. Far off I can just make out its trailing red jacklight riding on the surface of the water.

"It seems—no offense here—selfish," he says. "Like turning your back, walking away, and giving up. Here everybody else is trying to fix the schools, and you're just acquiescing, just *quitting*."

"I'm not quitting," I point out. "I'm a teacher."

"You're a quack, you mean," Bill says. "You won't send your kids to school. And anyway most homeschoolers aren't teachers—am I right? They don't have anything to do with schools. And why should they, anyway? Their kids aren't even in them. No, to me you're just plain selfish. If the schools go bad, you don't care. Let everybody else's children suffer but not your own—that's my read on you. Isolationist. Elitist. Un-American."

He's grinning now, beneath the brim of his hat, enjoying the sound of his own argument. But then gill-netters, generally speaking, are prone to contentious strife, straight-faced bluffers full of spleen and bile—in a universe of boats perpetually jock-eying for position such traits are vitally important.

"I know, I know," Bill presses on. "A lot of you home-schoolers are big-time believers in independence, freedom, self-sufficiency, the virtues that built the cities and farms, et cetera, et cetera. I know, you're more quintessentially American than the blind mass of ignorant conformists surrounding you on every side, right? The people at Burger King and in the shopping malls. Those yahoos and dunderheads who've given their children over to Big Government and The State in the form of Schools. You're better than they are, aren't you? Your independent, self-contained homeschool, in your head, is what American democracy is all about."

"I didn't say that," I reply. "I think a lot about this question of democracy. I—"

"The schools *are* democracy," Bill says. "You can't have democracy without 'em." He lifts his binoculars from off his chest and aims them at another fishing boat. "What kind of a country would this be—huh?—if everybody decided to homeschool? Tell you what you ought to do: Go back and read your Jefferson, President Democracy himself saying schools are the cornerstone of democracy. If you don't believe him, try Washington. This is the Father of Our Country saying to us—his last words before retiring to his slaves at Mount Vernon—that public schools serve the national interest, or something like that, anyway. On top of them," says Bill, "you've got your Horace Mann, founding father of the public school. Do you remember from your teacher-training days what he said, sounding like the Statue of Liberty? He said schools shouldn't distinguish between rich and poor, without money or price they ought to throw open their doors, spread the table of their bounty for all the children of the state, give me your tired, your poor, et cetera—not lofty enough for you, Dave? All right, let's see, who else can I give you? You libertarian progressives like to think John Dewey's your man, right? Like Dewey would approve of homeschooling? Hey, I've been reading Dewey. He's no more on your side than Dan Quayle. He—"

"Do you figure we're worse than private schoolers?" I say.

"Same kind of scum," Bill says.

"What about people who move to the suburbs looking for better public schools? You know, white flight? Are homeschoolers worse than they are?"

"*Real* bad scum," Bill says. "These folks hate themselves,

don't they? Misery, self-flagellation, guilt, that huge burden they carry on their backs for the decline of inner-city schools, their—"

"But wait," I answer, heating up now. "Inner-city schools *are* in decline. And urban and suburban schools aren't really equal—not really democratic—because they don't offer equal educational opportunity. Like in Texas, Bill. Wealthy school districts in Texas spend over seven thousand dollars on each student, but poor districts spend under three thousand. In Illinois the high is over twelve thousand dollars, and the low is just about two thousand. Rich schools have chemistry labs and cable-television hookups and computers and libraries filled with books. Poor schools—the ones poor children go to—have broken-down ventilation systems and smashed windows and cracked chalkboards. In a town like San Antonio you can visit schools so different from one another you'd think they were in different countries. A rich school will have a swimming pool and tennis courts; a poor one will have a playground with no basketball hoop, just a plastic bucket for a goal. In fact, the poor school won't even have what it takes to hire decent teachers. It can't attract them with good salaries and benefits the way the rich school can. It has to get by with dissatisfied teachers who are going to want to quit in a few years or move across town, where the salaries and benefits are better. How can a poor school do a good job of teaching when it can't afford to pay teachers competitively? And this in a country that likes to pride itself on its democratic schools. This kind of thing all across America. Sure there are exceptions, but the general rule is that the children of the middle class get a better shake than the children of the underclass in public schools. What's so democratic about that?"

"Nothing democratic," Bill says, shrugging. "I'll give you

seven points for all of that. Seven points but no more, Dave. You—"

"And what about private schools?" I ask. "The upper class, including our political leaders—our senators and presidents and representatives—has never been very interested in egalitarian education when it comes down to its own children. How can we pretend the playing field is really level when the rich have always gone to private schools?"

"All right, fine," Bill says. "So what if there are private schools for rich kids? It doesn't change what I'm trying to say one bit, and that's that the public schools are where democracy happens, where people learn to be citizens, where everybody mixes and pushes and pulls and struggles and debates and argues. A classroom is like a little congress where ideas get pushed around and negotiated and discussed. You're not doing that in your kitchen, are you? Learning how to engage in a public discourse on issues of real import? So your kids can be good citizens?"

"We are too doing that in the kitchen," I say. "Besides, your average classroom is more like a little Kremlin than a little congress, Bill. It's more like totalitarianism than democracy. There are bells and PA systems and student cards and hall passes and classrooms where you listen day in and day out to authoritarian voices. This one researcher, John Goodlad, sent notetakers into a thousand classrooms, and they found that less than two percent of instructional time was spent on discussions requiring students to offer an opinion about something. Another investigator, Ernest Boyer, did a lot of research for the Carnegie Foundation and came away with the conclusion that schools don't prepare children to become even *informed* citizens, not to mention *active* ones. Besides, on top of everything else, millions of children go to schools like Bainbridge where inequality is institutionalized by sorting students according to academic ability, which amounts to sorting them by social class. What's so democratic about that? What's so equal about that? After all the talk about schools as the land of opportunity, the place where the poor get the tools they need to escape from poverty, the fact remains that for the most part the poor remain poor from one generation to the next. And you know what? Public schools don't do very much to alter this state of affairs."

"That's ridiculous," Bill says. "Think of all the immigrants, like these Vietnamese, who come here and thank God for schools. Like the ones who live down there on the other side of Lovell—you know who I'm talking about? Oldest kid's studying to be a doctor now. Middle two are at the university in Seattle. Youngest one's pulling straight A's I bet at the high school where you work, isn't that right? Just about straight A's? Come on now," Bill insists. "Be logical about it. How could they do all that without schools? Where would those kids be—huh?—if they didn't have Bainbridge High? You think their parents could homeschool 'em?"

"Okay, I'll grant you that," I answer. "Plenty of immigrants have made good use of schools on their way to success in America. They've learned a new language and a new culture—all that's true. But there's also this, Bill. I once taught English as a second language to Indo-Chinese children at a Seattle public school, and a lot of those kids came to class with a zeal I wasn't responsible for. It came from their families, from the values their parents held out to them. Besides, not all immigrants flourish here, do they? A lot of them don't, but do we read about them in *Time* magazine or hear about them on television? The immigrant cum valedictorian makes good copy; the rest just don't. The myth is that schools provide equal opportunity to newcomers who've traveled here yearning to be free; the truth is that schools fail these immigrants for the same reasons they fail the urban poor. Immigrants are in the same boat as the poor people they're surprised to find already living here: They can't afford a house in the suburbs and have to fight for an education in underfunded, poorly managed, and just plain bad urban schools, while middle-class students learn under far better conditions. Even for immigrants, who usually are willing to take what they can get, our schools are not really democratic. The people you mentioned—the Nguyen family?—should be given a lot of credit for their accomplishments. Don't give schools all the praise for the fact they're doing so well here."

"Look," Bill says. "All right, I'll give it to you—schools aren't perfect. Schools have flaws. Everybody knows that. But just suppose everybody decided to do what you do. Suppose we were all a bunch of merry individualists off in our corners tending our own business with our heads buried in the sand. Huh? I'll tell you what: We wouldn't have a country. We'd be two hundred and fifty million individuals living on the same continent with zip in common, you know what I'm saying? I mean, right from the beginning we've got this big problem, we've got this rabid individualism, these salmon fishermen and loggers and ranchers—free, crazy, out-of-control guys. I mean, you read the Founding Fathers, like I've been doing lately, they were all worried about this point. They saw that we could end up with a lot of excess in a nation founded on worship of an individual's right to do whatever he pleases. It's crazy, this idea that anybody in America can do whatever he wants whenever he wants. Where's the nation in that? No, you've got to have schools, Mr. Schoolteacher. They're the *engine* of democracy, they're what make us better than the Brits; in fact, we revolted against the Brits so that we could get away from privately home-tutored snob aristocrats who don't care about egalitarian education—

let them eat cake! That's your attitude. No, schools are the great equalizer, kind of like death: They put everybody on the same level, give everyone the same shot at owning IBM one day, everybody gets the same deal."

"They don't all get the same deal," I say. "Our schools aren't equal. They're suburban or urban, rich or poor, they inspire docility and compliance. They—"

"They teach," Bill says. "They're supposed to teach every kid who comes through them. So school districts spend different amounts, and the system teaches kids to watch TV instead of think. Does that mean everybody should homeschool? We can try to make the schools better, maybe, instead of just dropping out."

"Sure we should make schools better. Of course we want them to work—who said otherwise? It's just that they're so far from working right now, Bill—I mean as far as democracy is concerned—that it seems like they've lost sight of their purpose. You're the one who mentioned Dewey. Dewey felt schools should have explicit democratic goals on top of their academic and social ones. He wanted students not only to make school decisions but to participate in implementing them; he wanted the school to be a democratic community where students expressed their wills. Dewey figured schools would be places where upper-crust kids would engage in ordinary occupations— plumbing, carpentry, electrical work—so that they wouldn't turn out to be snobs, you see, and to get them ready for adulthood. If he were alive today, he'd be sick at heart, Bill. He'd see the schools as a betrayal of his vision. School kids have no role in decision making; they don't participate in manual occupations; they're tracked, sorted, graded, and evaluated— something like the way we treat beef cattle. Their school experience is so far removed from Dewey's democratic vision—

from any thoughtful person's democratic vision—that if we stand back for a moment and ponder it, it may seem more like preparation for totalitarianism than anything else."

"Are you a Commie?" Bill asks.

"Hitler would have asked the same," I say, "and Hitler would not have been joking. You know what? A totalitarian state 'will give its youth to no one, but will itself take youth and give to youth its own education and its own upbringing.' Those are Hitler's very words, Bill."

"So now I'm in the same league with Hitler," Bill says. "Hitler, the devil, and Manuel Noriega. Will you stop babbling already? We're already agreed about schools being messed up—get that through your head. We're *agreed* there. What I want to know is what we'd do without 'em. Okay? You got that? Where'd we be without 'em? What would we be if everybody were insane like you and kept his kids locked up in the house?"

But we are interrupted just then by a disembodied voice from the radio set, another fisherman from down the sound, somebody, apparently, Bill knows. He lifts the transmitter to the corner of his mouth. "Yeah I got you done just got the bug out of my squelch," Bill says evenly.

"Well, yeah, I got you good now. Ya done any done good?"

"Well, one good shiny, Doug, you know, twenty or so on the tide turn but don't know what's doin' now."

"Same," Doug says. "Just about."

"Yeah, well, done got me a deckhand," Bill says. "Got to get good this night for his split, anyway."

"'Sit Ray you got there? Buddy's Ray?"

"Dave," Bill says. "'Sa new guy. Teacher. Been drivin' me crazy too."

"Teacher?" Doug says. "Toss him overboard."

"You don't answer my question I'll take Doug's advice," Bill says a few minutes later, grinning. "I want to know where we'd be if everybody followed your lead and just 'cause he felt like it yarded his kids out of school." Bill pops the top off a can of Pepsi, rests his feet on a plastic float, and drinks heartily with his head thrown back, gazing up into the stars.

"I don't advocate that," I explain. "I don't say homeschooling's for everybody. But don't you think it ought to be an option for anybody who wants to try it? Don't you think parents should get themselves involved in the education of their children? I don't see how that's elitist, Bill. I don't see what's un-American about it."

"You know this guy Jim Brownell?" Bill says. "Down at the salmon pens? He's got two girls, homeschools them both, figures it's some kind of civil disobedience, like refusing to pay taxes or register for the draft. He thinks homeschooling's some kind of *statement*, like the schools are so fascist and undemocratic that he can't bring himself to take part in them. So you know what? He turns his back and walks around acting like he's truly American, a true democratic citizen, because he sees through the fascist conspiracy of schools. I mean, come on," Bill says. "The guy turns his back on the public schools and walks around acting like he's *God* or something."

"But not all homeschoolers are like that," I say. "You ought to judge them one at a time, Bill. A lot of them are trying to work with the schools. They come forward at public forums and school-board meetings, they—"

"Oh, come on," Bill says. "Most of you homeschoolers aren't hanging around the superintendent giving him an earful, are you? You're too busy carting your offspring to 4-H meetings and rock-club field trips and the like. Are you trying to tell me homeschoolers are this driving force in improving public education? It just isn't so, and you know it. Nobody's listening to you."

"You're wrong," I say. "There are districts all over the country where homeschoolers are an integral part of things. They've worked to set up public-school programs that involve parents, families, their communities. They've stayed interested in the education of everybody's kids. Jim Brownell isn't everybody."

"He's most people," Bill says.

"Look," I say. "There are a lot of school districts that have begun to recognize the need for education in the home. They're starting what are essentially homeschooling programs. There's this home-instruction program for preschool kids in the New Orleans schools that helps single mothers living in housing projects figure out how to teach their own. The district sends tutors in—they're neighbors, Bill, drawn directly from the community—not to teach the kids themselves but to teach their mothers how to teach them. The program is so successful that there are now dozens like it across the country. It's a good program. It works. The mothers get some of their confidence and pride back. They feel good about being teachers to their children. A lot of them take up working on their own education as a result. Too bad that right now the program is just for preschool children. It could do a lot of good for older kids, too, especially with the support and approval of public schools. It—"

"Won't happen," Bill says sliding forward in his deck chair. "People want democratic schools. They don't want the neighbor banging on the door saying, 'Hey, good morning. Let me show you how to teach Junior long division. By the way, got any coffee? What's for breakfast—har har.' "

"Maybe not," I answer. "But look, there are a lot of ways to do things. Educators in Indianapolis get to parents where they work, with workshops on teaching children to read. In Minneapolis there's something called the Success by Six Program; it helps parents get their kids set for school. San Francisco has its Quality Education Project, where parents sign pledges to take more responsibility for their children's education. Even the federal government has proposed a program—called Parents As Teachers—meant to help out people on welfare. It will train them to teach their kids the same way parenting classes train expectant mothers and fathers. The point is that sooner or later we're going to have to involve whole families if we're going to improve education. And we're going to have to find ways to reach out to families that aren't working very well too. That's where public education can play an important role. Rather than sending poor kids to bad schools, we ought to be working with their families—it's the only way that can work."

"People'll still want democratic schools," Bill insists. "Say what you want about all these programs. Without democratic schools we wouldn't have a country, would we? What kind of country would we be?"

"What kind of country are we now? Maybe we ought to keep in mind that what we're after is a democratic country, not democratic schools. And right now we don't have a democratic country, partly because education isn't equal. We won't have it until we come face-to-face with a statement I hear all the time from schoolteachers: that education *begins at home*. Go ahead and fix all the unfairness of our school system; you'll never have a fair society without helping families to educate their kids. Because as things now stand education happens sometimes in the homes of the upper and middle classes but far less often in the homes of poor people. And the poor are going to stay poor and outside the mainstream of democracy until we do something about that."

Bill is silent for a moment. "You sound like a politician," he says. "Michael Dukakis or somebody."

We watch another gill-netter motor past, his spotlight grazing across Bill's net gently before sweeping ahead to the south. Yawning, then standing, then yawning again, Bill stretches his back muscles. "Time to pick some fish," he says. "All done chewing the fat."

But later when I am rinsing the deck clean, washing the fish gurry out of the scupper holes—and Bill has dropped thirty silvers onto the ice in his hold—he asks me what I know, if anything, about the North Pacific Fishery Management Council. He says that they intend to do to the Alaska fisherman what they did to the small farmer. He says that the little guy is on his way out, that everybody in the industry is overcapitalized, that "the proverbial shit is about to hit the proverbial fan," that a lot of guys are going to lose everything. Take the one-day halibut opener, Bill says, it might not be perfect but at least it's an opener. Now the federal pencil pushers want to regulate everything: safety goggles, motorcycle helmets, seat-belt laws, first-aid kits. . . .

"Sure," I say, "but without some kind of regulation the fish'll disappear. Then where would you guys be?"

At 5:00 A.M., with the light coming up and the mist rising off Puget Sound, Bill and I are still arguing about it beneath a fading quarter moon.

3

Homeschoolers Among Others

But what about your children's socialization? is a question I am far more likely to field than *How well are they learning?* It is also a far more perplexing question, chiefly because there are many definitions of a proper socialization but also because objective measures of socialization, however defined, are of dubious value at best. No one really knows what socialization is or how to identify it in the lives of children—homeschooled children and all others. Despite the best efforts of sociologists and anthropologists, authoritative answers to common questions about socialization elude schoolers and homeschoolers both. *But what about your children's socialization?* is a riddle that ought to perplex every parent.

Yet the question is often posed to me by people with something very clear in mind: maintaining our fragile social consensus. My father, for example, a thoughtful man in his early sixties and a great believer in our public schools, counts himself proudly among them. A criminal attorney, son of an immigrant father, he worries that the vast diversity of the United States implies real dangers if we are not vigilant about or are unresponsive to the forces of fragmentation—and homeschooling is a significant one, he adds. He sees it as inevitably contributing to the gradual demise of our social unity and public schools as our most vital institution for creating and sustaining this unity. Homeschooling, he insists, is a divisive force that tears at the social fabric. Like cultists, survivalists, and religious fanatics, homeschoolers are, in his view of things, symptomatic of the breakdown of our society.

For others the socialization question is a far less idealistic one, aimed not at the cohesiveness of society but at the competitive social advantage of individuals. Here, *What about your children's socialization?* means, in essence, *How do you expect them to understand people well enough to get ahead in the world if you don't send them to school?* The focus is on the perception and insight of children, their adroitness and skill at reading others, and the assumption is that school is a necessary prerequisite to this sort of social mastery. About this I am never much prone to argue, for certainly we learn a great deal about others whenever and wherever we interact with them: at home, on the playground, on Main Street, on the job, at church, at Girl Scout meetings, in classrooms. Whether we learn to interact well, however—in a manner conducive to sustaining a society all of us find worth living in—is another question altogether, one worth considering with particular care in any discussion of our public schools.

But what about your sons' socialization? is for others among our schooling friends a question about their current social life. They simply want to know if our boys have any friends to speak of and are concerned that homeschooling must mean by definition a great diminishing of social opportunity. For them homeschooling evokes sad isolation, a world devoid of intimate friendships and composed chiefly of loneliness. In their mind's eye they see our boys hunkered down at our kitchen table, silently toiling along with their pencils, friendless, isolated, with one of us, perhaps, hovering over their shoulders, but with no one their own age present. In asking the socialization question they ask us to justify the diminished role they assume peers play in the lives of our children and to defend what they see as our intentional limiting of their social universe.

For others the socialization question is about whether Robin and I can accept the inevitability of our sons' movement away from us. Here, *What about your sons' socialization?* means *What about weaning yourselves from them and allowing them to make their own path through life?* Their assumption is that the intimacy between parent and child inherent in the home-schooling life is potentially obsessive, unhealthy, sentimental, perhaps even dangerous to the child's developing psyche. They worry that as social beings our sons will strangle under the weight of our relentless presence, birdlings never pushed from the nest, so to speak, and forever limited—perhaps forever neurotic too—as a consequence.

Finally there is the set of social realists who ask, *But what about your sons' socialization?* and mean by it that life in a mass society requires—for better or worse—a mass form of socialization such as school. Socialization is for them the process by which the individual is shaped to the needs of society and by which the individual comes to see his own fulfillment in social terms, and this, they say, is what schools offer. The point of view here is, I think, ironic, given that the society they are committed to sustaining is one clearly founded on the primacy of the individual, who cannot thrive, and thus benefit his fellow citizen, when his talents and desires are subsumed by a set of larger social concerns. Finally we must ask these realists to define just what the needs of society are, how they might be balanced and even met by attention to the needs of individuals, and just what—or who—they mean by society, and we should do all this before we accept the proposition that children should attend mass institutions of education chiefly because "society" needs them to.

The socialization question, then, asks a great variety of things and demands from homeschoolers a great variety of answers. Researchers have thus far not been much help—in part because socialization is so difficult to measure, in part because the sum of research to date is astonishingly limited. While schoolchildren over the years have been subjected to a wide array of tests and studies on personality, "self-concept," and "social adjustment," homeschooled children have remained unscrutinized in these regards, with a few exceptions. John Wesley Taylor V's 1986 study compared the "self-concept"—an ambiguous term—of homeschooled children to that of their conventionally schooled peers and found it to be "significantly higher." About half of the 224 homeschoolers examined scored at or above the 91st percentile on something called the Piers-Harris global scale, which seeks to measure "the central core of personality." Taylor concluded that the results might best be explained by homeschoolers' higher achievement and mastery levels, by their independent study characteristics, by one-on-one tutoring in the homeschool environment—academic explanations all—or by high levels of parental interest and communication, homeschoolers' relative independence from peers, their relatively strong sense of responsibility and comparatively low anxiety levels. He also concluded that "insofar as self-concept is a reflector of socialization, it would appear that few homeschooling children are socially deprived. Critics of the home school should not urge self-concept and socialization rationales. These factors apparently favor homeschoolers over the conventionally schooled population."

Linda Montgomery's 1988 study on the leadership skills of homeschooled children suggests that homeschoolers are not isolated from their age peers and are as likely as conventionally schooled children to be involved in church activities, community-service work, music and dance lessons, and youth clubs such as Scouts and 4-H; they are even more likely to hold down jobs. (Nearly 80 percent of the homeschoolers in Montgomery's study, interestingly enough, ran their own businesses, such as delivering papers, mowing lawns, baby-sitting, or caring for neighbors' houses; over half took on such volunteer projects in their communities as visiting hospitals and nursing homes or doing chores or baby-sitting for needy families.) Montgomery's data followed on the heels of a 1986 Washington State survey in which homeschoolers reported a median twenty to twenty-nine hours a month involvement in organized community activities and the same amount of time in contact with other children outside their immediate families. In short, homeschoolers spend plenty of time with other children approximately their own age, though not as much as schoolchildren do; the assumption that they are socially isolated is not substantiated by research.

Yet these studies, together, are nearly all we have, and they do not yield much insight into the socialization of homeschooled children nor are they entirely reliable. It appears homeschoolers spend plenty of time with people outside their immediate families, are "well adjusted," and have a "high self-concept," but beyond that the usefulness of the research is extremely limited. Far more needs to be done.

Socialization has been variously defined as the process of adapting to currently accepted mores and conventions, as the process by which all members of society come to share a common experience, or are adapted to the needs of their society or assimilated into groups so as to become socially active. Among teachers the term is further muddled by our twofold interest in defining it: On the one hand we are concerned about socialization in its own right, entirely divorced from academic considerations; on the other we want to know as much as possible about the connection between socialization and learning. We want to find out whatever we can about the relationship between social life and academic results, chiefly from a concern for improving both.

But teachers must also confront a daily dilemma that derives squarely from the social realities of schools. Consider that at my school, as at many, students are sorted not only by age—so that they spend their class hours among close peers in this regard—but also by a tracking system that categorizes them according to academic ability. (Bainbridge High's tracking system is self-selecting, so students can decide for themselves where they fit in—Basic, Regular, or Honors. Despite this, movement between tracks is severely limited.) Teachers can do little or nothing to alter these built-in social divisions, for schools are nearly as inflexible in the social sense as they are in the academic. In fact, during recent curriculum meetings our English department has acknowledged the academic benefits of tracking while regretting its adverse social impact, and this, the literature about tracking suggests, is an educational dilemma nationwide.

The convenient method—and the obvious one given the enormous administrative task at hand—of enrolling schoolchildren according to their place of residence means that schools are often relatively homogenous places with student populations composed of individuals from similar ethnic and socioeconomic backgrounds. Where this is not the case the practice of tracking often ensures that students from different backgrounds will not mix in ways that are meaningful or constructive. Schools with diverse student populations are sometimes, ironically, places where young people learn the art of engaging those unlike themselves in superficial, dishonest, or self-serving ways—or, more likely, of not engaging them at all. Ten years ago I taught at a public high school much celebrated for its diversity, an inner-city school with a voluntary busing program widely hailed as a model of integration. As it turned out my Advanced Placement Senior English class was uniformly composed of upper-middle-class white students who were quite frank in discussing the mechanisms they had devised for fending off others in the school. I was chagrined to discover how well they were learning to circumvent those unlike themselves via subtle stratagems and deliberate manipulations—enrolling only in certain classes, frequenting safe havens and private corners for lunch, leaving the building quickly when day was done, or staying on for only those extracurricular activities they participated in exclusively (the school newspaper, for example). I am often told that at school we learn to get along with everybody or that at school we learn how to function among strangers, but those who would make much of schools as the breeding ground of social understanding should think again about the adult world schools have helped create. Shall we give schools credit for holding the line while the fabric of society unravels around us, or shall we name schools as a contributor?

Young people at Bainbridge High find themselves immersed in an enormously complicated social context. The sheer body of fellow students is too large to be gotten hold of, a somewhat disquieting army of others who simultaneously threaten their sense of well-being and invite their instinctive curiosity. Unprepared by nature for life in a hive—they are not, after all, bees or ants but rather the heirs of an enduring tribal structure that by definition limited one's social universe—they armor themselves within a cadre of intimate friends, what Bainbridge students call "cliques" with mixed emotions: On the one hand they have created this key feature of their social landscape out of need and for legitimate psychological reasons; on the other they recognize its ruinous implications and the general injustice of their social invention. They partake of it and despise it simultaneously, bemoan the pains it brings them but hold it close to their hearts.

Bainbridge, like all schools, has its social divisions—jocks and burnouts, as they are called in some places, or collegiates and greasers or socs and hoods or, as they are sometimes referred to here, preppies and stoners. Many of my colleagues attribute the existence of these divisions to forces beyond the control of our school, suggesting that they arise from our community's broader class distinctions (white-collar and blue-collar). But the school is at least as responsible as other forces for their formation and their implications. These divisions are encouraged at Bainbridge, not explicitly but implicitly and in ways that go far beyond the academic practice of tracking. This is not because Bainbridge is an intentionally cruel place, but rather because it is a large institution where children must shape an identity for themselves through symbols, clothing, language, and mannerisms that suggest an affinity for a distinct set of others—otherwise they are lost, adrift, anonymous faces in a crowd.

Friendship at my school, as in adult organizations, gives an individual social leverage (going to the right parties, as they say, or hanging out with the right people) and is thus far too often merely expedient. The highly competitive atmosphere at Bainbridge, nurtured by its athletic program, by its system of grades, by tracking, and by the structure of classroom life (and finally by the built-in social mechanics of the institution, its cheerleaders and student-body officers, its club chairpersons and basketball team captains, its honor roll and senior poll and class valedictorians)—it all inspires a daily tension and makes of school a "social combat zone," as one recent graduate put it. (Telling in this regard is the now pervasive use of the term *loser* at Bainbridge to describe, quite indiscreetly, those who are vanquished in the furious social war of school.) In fact, many young people I know graduate with a sense of relief, thankful that the long battle for school status is behind them, that the closed, neurotic universe they have inhabited for twelve years among an essentially fixed body of contesting peers can at last be left to those who follow. They roll their eyes on hearing it said that "these are the best years of your lives," or—to make use of yet another graduation day cliché that conceals behind it the realities of school—"your days among good high-school friends you will remember always and cherish."

A counter argument I often hear is that the competitive life of schools is a necessary prerequisite to the competitive economic lives adults lead. But this is the argument of people who don't distinguish between social health and financial success, between sound relationships and the necessities of economics, between the welfare of society and the mechanics of capitalism. Those who assert that we are condemned to social struggle in order for our economic system to work assert by extension that we must lead unhealthy social lives. Schools should not be arranged so as to foment a perpetual and relentless social strife merely to prepare people to perpetuate the same arrangement when, one day, they go to work in the world. On the contrary, we should want our schools to aspire to something better.

Yet preparation for life in a competitive economy **is** built into the very structure of schools, and insofar as they allow one to adapt to it we should be relatively pleased with their performance. The watching of clocks, the strictness of the schedule, the expectation of punishment for being late or for behavior that lies outside certain guidelines—it all corresponds to the complex social world many children will enter into as working adults. Yet while they might enter into it successfully as a result of schooling, they may at the same time have left behind their desire to improve it—and what is more, they may also have left behind the imaginative individualism, the inventiveness and flair, that once contributed much to America's economic life and which is now required to reinvigorate it. It is a smallness of mind and spirit, finally, that asks schools to prepare students, in the social sense, for their roles in the current American workplace and to teach them implicitly to struggle with one another while simultaneously suppressing their individuality. Do we, indeed, want our schools to train yet another generation in a brand of social competition that is in danger of permeating our lives so thoroughly that we are, both as individuals and collectively, permanently damaged by it? This is not what our schools were intended to do nor is it what we want from them.

In theory the twentieth-century public school was meant to be a model not of economic life but of the larger community in which it was set, a microcosm of the world the child would inhabit as citizen, not as worker. "When the school introduces and trains each child of society into membership within such a little community," wrote John Dewey, "saturating him with the spirit of service, and providing him with the instruments of effective self-direction, we shall have the deepest and best guarantee of a larger society which is worthy, lovely, and harmonious." This design, however, was supplanted by another that was more practical given the logistical problems of large schools and more realistic given the central facts of our society—preparation for economic life instead of life in a community.

Today we think of schools in some of the same ways we think of hospitals or prisons, as buildings housing scores of people but with only a very limited connection to the world outside their walls. They are artifices, intentionally constructed *models* of adult economic life, that cut children off from the social web of their communities. Having passed their formative years chiefly among their peers in a world devoid of the very old and very young, a highly structured world best characterized as competitive and cliquish, they are ill prepared for membership in their own communities even if adequately prepared to function in our economy. (In many instances they are ill prepared even in this latter regard; business leaders constantly complain about the incompetence, for example, of Harvard Business School graduates.) Our schools simply do not function in the social sense as anything like Dewey's guarantors of a worthy, lovely, and harmonious society. Good things happen in schools, yes, but they happen against the odds, in spite of schools' structure, and because human beings in them continue to insist on the good in spite of everything.

Homeschooling, on the other hand, is certainly no cure-all for our social ills, and if practiced without vision or without sensitivity to the nation's social needs, may, in fact, do great harm. A homeschooled child can indeed be isolated, as critics claim, with little social life beyond his family; he can be socially inept both as a youth and an adult, permanently troubled by the obsessive nature of his relationship with his parents, lonely, confused, and at odds with the world in a way that frustrates him daily. His enforced aloneness can bring him excruciating pain, and in a home that provides him with little opportunity to interact with peers it can constitute a form of child abuse. At its worst homeschooling can evoke the horrifying image of a child confined to his parents' home for years—like Boo Radley in *To Kill a Mockingbird* or one of those abused children we sometimes read about who have been locked in attics from infancy.

Homeschooling can be a social danger, too, when it is chiefly a strategy for narrowing the child's experience for political, social, or religious purposes. I point out those various cultists and extremists who seek, through homeschooling, to indoctrinate their children into their worldview while denying them access to others. American parents, of course, have the right to mold the values and premises of their children—this right is also a responsibility no one should relinquish to the public schools without deliberate forethought—but most would agree, too, about the importance of nurturing in their children an open mind and open heart. This is an obligation in a pluralistic society, a value, I think, we share as a people and one of those areas where the rights of individuals and the needs of society collide.

My father might say, and I would agree, that some form of national consensus about values is so vital to America that even given our dedication to the principle of diversity our survival as a people is in the long run predicated on it. One function of schools as they were originally conceived was to nurture this process of national consensus building and to help shape a society based on common principles. My father's fear that homeschooling undercuts this process is justified when we consider some of the bad that can happen: Homeschoolers can be propagandized, even brainwashed, by parents who have no commitment to the values of a pluralistic society. The risk in promoting homeschooling is that we may promote bigotry and narrow-mindedness, too, meanwhile undermining an institution that could be vital to the battle against these forces—our public-education system.

But schools have not been effective agents of consensus

building. Nor must a society in which families take primary responsibility for education—a homeschooling society, if you will, based on cooperation between families and government—inevitably become fragmented. On the contrary, homeschooling can do much to promote the process of building a national consensus, beginning, of course, by inspiring a consensus about the importance of family life. A homeschooling society might also nurture the kind of independent-minded, critical electorate our republic now desperately needs; it might infuse our tired democracy with a new, grass-roots energy. Homeschooling could inspire a broader commitment to community service and allow for the maintenance of different cultural traditions within the American setting. It could also generate a new respect for diversity in values, pursuits, and principles—and for the process of education itself. All of this, of course, is speculative and utopian. It is also worth considering.

Schools have lost their social effectiveness in part because so much has changed since they were first inserted into the American landscape. We now have, for better or worse, television, newspapers, magazines, and the cinema exerting themselves as powerful forces from which we take our cues as a people. If we have a consensus at all, it is generated and sustained primarily by these forces—they do the job given over to schools in the century preceding this one. Whether we like it or not our schools have become increasingly irrelevant as a positive social mechanism, and far more powerful tools now exist to take their place. This is worrisome, chiefly because the new tools have been so thoroughly misused and used for the wrong ends; I do not celebrate them. Nevertheless, it remains true that schools cannot effectively build consensus in part because they have been supplanted by new forces they can neither compete with nor fend off. If our consensus as a nation now comes from media, and if this concerns us as a people—it rightly should—we should be willing to admit as a corollary that our schools as a social force are diminished by it, perhaps diminished so greatly that we have no choice but to demand of them vigorous and fundamental change.

My sons may lack the experience of classroom hierarchy and large-scale competition, but this does not mean that by extension they are doomed to lifelong social failure. Since they are not confined for long hours each day to a world composed almost exclusively of peers they have opportunities for intimacy with people of all sorts and all ages. They might play chess at a local nursing home with a veteran of the Battle of Iwo Jima who displays for them both his wounds and his medals or rake leaves on Tuesday morning with the neighbor from England who subsequently takes them into her home and regales them with tales of her own war years over biscuits and chocolate milk. These are more than history lessons; they are instruction in the intricacies of people, too—people who are not their peers.

My sons' relationships to others, moreover, are not damaged by the forces of institutional life—competition, tracking, cliques, social hierarchy—that hamper my students at Bainbridge High School. Thus they seem to me far more likely to develop a lifelong empathy and compassion for others not much like themselves. This is not to say that schoolchildren must grow up to lack compassion but that life in the real world of human beings is a training ground superior to schools in this regard. Living as an integral part of a community, among the elderly, store clerks, gardeners, carpenters, plumbers, mechanics, and electricians in their world, "homeschoolers" (here the sense of a misnomer is especially acute) are apt to develop a sensitive social understanding and a sophisticated feeling for the lives of others as they are lived on a daily basis. This insight, if we are foremost concerned with the advantage children gain over others via their social understanding, will certainly serve them well as adults, even as it serves well the larger society in which they live and to which they will inevitably contribute.

One of the most worthy aspects of school life is the meaningful relationship that sometimes develops between individual students and teachers. This is a much celebrated phenomenon, and rightly so, because it brings young people together with adults in a way that sidesteps the general rigidity and impersonality of schools. Many of us have poignant memories of teachers—memories, if we are honest, that we sometimes exaggerate. (Even as we speak of them, claiming Ms. White's or Mr. Brown's enormous influence, we are aware of an element of dissembling. It is often only in retrospect that we conjure their impact or wax lyrical over just how much they meant to us.) Nevertheless, wonderful relationships do develop between teachers and students, primarily because young people seek them out and even beg unconsciously for them. It is clear to me at Bainbridge High just how much I am needed by certain children, needed in a way that goes beyond academics, amateur psychology, even mere friendship, chiefly because I am an adult in their world who is there consistently and at work. (This *at work* notion is important. Children are often far removed from the mysteries of what their parents do for money and when asked are prone to throw up their hands, shrug, and confess they don't know. Naturally, then, they gravitate toward teachers, who work among them while their parents—most other adults for that matter—are of necessity working far away.)

Schoolchildren may be openly and consciously obsessed with their peers, but their unconscious desperation for meaningful relationships with adults can be plainly seen in their eyes. The ones who single me out enter my classroom before the others or come in at lunch or after school, somewhat tentatively but with hopeful expressions. They appear almost always with some avowed purpose, some express mission they are zealous about —clarification of a note I have written in the margin of an essay on war and bravery or elucidation of a point made the day before about a poem by Robinson Jeffers—and I am pleased when they do not excuse themselves once this pretext is out of the way. We speak of college plans or life at home or books read over the summer; we trade ideas about any number of things, and as we do I am sure to note, with satisfaction, *their* satisfaction with these discussions. Many of these visitors, furthermore, are students from past years or past semesters who have no interest in stroking the grade book or in nurturing false goodwill. They simply recognize their affinity for me and seek me out because of it. It is an aspect of school life I cherish as much as they do. Their maturation and growth in large part depends on the development of these sorts of bonds with adults and on the degree to which these relationships develop fully. Yet the structure of school life, which is vast and impersonal, usually prevents these attachments from deepening in a way that provides for the needs of children. There are only so many teachers to go around for hundreds, even thousands, of young people, and our relationships are anyway so much hampered by the authoritarian prerequisites of mass instruction (which force teachers to cultivate the straight face, the hard edge, the impersonal persona) that it is often difficult for us to understand one another or to see one another's humanity. Again, it seems to me that these rare, meaningful relationships are achieved against the odds, as so much else is in schools.

In the past a child found adults through apprenticeships or tribal institutions or because small communities retained a natural integrity that led children into the presence of mentors.

Schools have been less successful than any of these arrangements in part because they are inflexible, in part because in school students bear the same relationship to teachers that sheep do to shepherds. The numbers, ultimately, don't work out for individuals.

Many homeschooling parents recognize instinctively that their children need relationships with other adults and go to great lengths to ensure these relationships are cultivated. While schooling parents we know are prone to worry that perhaps they need to spend more time with their children, their homeschooling counterparts are prone to feel that perhaps they need to spend less. Both concerns are natural and lead to healthy outcomes, yet it remains true that too often schoolchildren never develop meaningful relationships with adults who are not their parents. Ironically, it is homeschooled children who stand the better chance of moving beyond the home and into the lives of adult mentors. A local homeschooler, for example, has apprenticed herself to an island artist; another works with a jeweler one day, a marine biologist the next. In Michigan a third interns in a costume museum where the curators are three older women. A fourth, Britt Barker, spent two months in Canada with a wildlife artist and a museum biologist, studying endangered species; at sixteen she traveled to the Appennines to track wolves with a team of field researchers. Finally, Kristine Beck left her Alaska home at age fourteen to live and work in an exotic-animal breeding compound thousands of miles away in Florida. All were able to do these things precisely because they were not confined by institutions and could move about with freedom in the world, finding adults in their communities and beyond who have and who are what they need. Perhaps more interestingly, they did them because they have parents who let them go—in part out of the fear that they have been too attached, in part because these parents have passed enough meaningful and fulfilling time with their children. Homeschooling parents never worry about "quality time" and are thus well able, many of them, to let go of their children at an early age, when the children need this letting go. The depth and intimacy of the homeschooling arrangement allows parents to feel right about making way for significant experiences and significant adults outside the family circle.

Their children are also well prepared for relationships with adult mentors because they have thoroughly explored the territory of their parents and because they haven't learned to be alienated, generally, from adults. By contrast, I am often dismayed at how painfully neurotic most schoolchildren are in their behavior toward me, how inadequate they are to the task of meeting me as an adult living in their world. They are stilted, uncomfortable, fawning, nervous, irritable, defensive, uncertain, angry—precisely what they have learned to be in their years at school from embattled teachers struggling to create order in the classroom. I am not a human being to these students but a teacher. I represent an overwhelming, oppressive bureaucracy that has been busily depersonalizing them for years. (A perennially favorite song among Bainbridge students—one that has all the force of an anthem—is Pink Floyd's enormously popular "The Wall": "*Hey! Teacher! Leave the kids alone . . .*" it shouts.) One result is that they end up turning, sometimes with desperation, to peers who share their worldview and condition, peers who by rights ought to play a significant role in their lives but who nevertheless cannot do everything, cannot, for example, act as mentors, guides, or role models. These children are missing something fundamental, some primary and essential relationship to older people, and they do not get it in part because of how schools shape their interactions with adults.

The peer orientation of schoolchildren is often discussed and often worried about. Many of my students' parents instinctively recognize that the obsessive nature of their children's friendships is both dangerous and unhealthy. They speak of their children as "running in packs" on weekend nights, "obsessively" fielding "trivial phone calls," "cruising around aimlessly on Friday evenings," and "wasting all their time with the same crowd." Yet peer obsessiveness and the clique mentality are the natural responses of children to mass schooling, which in essence removes adults from their lives or rather puts them there at a ratio of one to thirty and in an authoritarian role not entirely conducive to the forming of meaningful relationships. Is it any wonder that our children tend to shun adults and instead pursue one another relentlessly not only at school but outside of it as well? Their need for adults, unfulfilled and frustrated, urges them to grasp even more obsessively—this is a staple of psychological theory about adolescent peer dependency—at what their peers have to offer in consolation. Yet while they do indeed need their peers, and while most parents are happy to see them find and develop peer friendships, it is generally clear to both parent (consciously) and child (unconsciously) that something is out of balance, out of sync, in their social universe.

Homeschooling, when practiced carefully, allows children to develop a more balanced set of relationships not only with peers and with adults in their communities but with their families and parents as well. It gives them many adults in many contexts as opposed to the student-teacher relationship, which can be excellent but more often lacks intimacy and has behind it the shadow of the teacher's red grade book. Homeschoolers, generally speaking, are not only less vulnerable to peer pressure than their public-school counterparts but less peer obsessed and thus better able to enter into vital relationships with adults.

They are, in my experience, quite often mature and independent young people, confident in their values (which, significantly, are not necessarily values imitative of their parents', as certain critics of homeschooling fear, and also not thoughtlessly imitative of their peers', as we might legitimately fear of schoolchildren) and well enough grounded in the worldview of their parents that they are able to move away from it and them with comfort, assurance, and ease. They are likely to develop close relationships with siblings of the sort school friendships often undercut: Homeschooled siblings must live and learn with one another, and the intensity and meaning of their relationship, its daily depth and fragility, become the standard for future relationships. Without the chaotic background of hundreds of peers that ultimately distorts the social lives of school students, allowing carelessness and cruelty to creep in, homeschoolers are able to nurture the health of a few intimate and important connections. Like all children they develop friendships with others of like minds—with other homeschoolers, private schoolers, public schoolers, cousins, siblings—and while these friendships are apt to be fraught with many of the same difficulties and tribulations we find among schoolchildren, they are also not troubled by school's social web, its cliques, rumors, and relentless gossip, its shifting alliances and expedient betrayals, which all produce dark complications. They have the potential to be *whole* in the sense that at the center of their universe lie not primarily their age peers but instead the communities in which they live and the families from which they spring.

The forces of socialization are complex and subtle, and we should be wary of attributing too much that is good or bad to either homeschooling or public schools. *But what about your children's socialization?* is a question that takes in a variety of forces, including family, school, community, television, the cinema, even magazines and newspapers. Nevertheless, my students' parents have often expressed, in our conferences together, dismay at how *school* has shaped their children, and this dismay needs close examining. It is part of the growing alienation they feel from their children, who gradually become estranged from them as they become ever more deeply immersed in the universe of their school peers—an alienation parents erroneously conclude is a "natural" part of their children's growing up, a necessary prerequisite to their independent adulthood. This distance, though, is far from natural, and the dismay parents feel about it ought not to be repressed. There is nothing natural about children obsessed with their peers and acutely attuned to a preadult commercial culture that usurps their attention (MTV, Nintendo, fashion magazines, teen cinema)—a world to which they become acutely attuned in part via their peer relationships. Many parents react by trying to stem the tide, but this is a sea that will not be turned back and that has behind it the force of years. It begins at least as early as kindergarten, when the child is introduced into an institutional life among peers and uprooted from family and community.

What about your children's socialization? is a question homeschooling parents are often asked as if surely they can have no decent answer. Perhaps it is time for the parents of schoolchildren to begin to ask themselves the same question in tones of equal concern.

4

My Father Comes to Class

One day last April a student of mine, a boy in the back row named Matthew Brush, rose during a discussion about supporting evidence for thesis statements and announced that he was going to leave.

For three years I had known him to be unpredictable and moody, a budding narcissist who shamelessly took much time with his hair—gelling it into dark curls and waves in the style of a London New Wave Romantic—a slight, angry, and acute young man who preferred to sulk in a far corner with his head down and rarely spoke unless it was to say things bitter, challenging, surly, or blunt, but generally, in a cynical way, very much on the mark.

"You're leaving?" I ask. "How come?"

"Because I'm not learning anything, okay?" he answers. "I don't have, like, any *reason* to be here. I heard about this in Thompson's last year."

I explain to Matt my professional obligation to report his absence to the attendance office; I remind him that the school has a policy regarding unexcused absences that is not to his personal advantage. I ask him if he in fact wants to leave given the potential consequences—a parent conference, an after-school detention—at hand when he walks out the door.

"No problem," Matt Brush says. "Go ahead and report me. That isn't going to be any problem."

It comes to me, watching him—his eyes particularly, their gleeful assurance—what Matthew Brush has in mind. Today is, by no coincidence at all, his long-awaited eighteenth birthday. I know this because he'd made a point of announcing it, loudly and with an unapologetic, self-celebratory brusqueness, on his way in at the beginning of the period. And, as we both know, the school has a special attendance policy for eighteen-year-olds, one grounded in a fundamental truth of state law: Matt is, for most legal purposes in Washington, a kind of adult, and thus entitled to a whole host of adult freedoms.

In other words, he no longer needed his parents' permission to come or go, stay or leave: If he wanted to, the law said, he could excuse himself for "personal reasons" and nobody, nothing in the world, could prevent him.

I smile, begin to bow, gesture in a courtly manner toward the open door, in something of the manner of a fencer who has been pricked at the heart. "Touché, then, Matt," I say.

Matt whips the gelled hair from his eyes. "Whatever," he says. "Touché or whatever. But I know my rights."

He strides up the row, swivels toward the doorway. "Goodbye, Matt," I say. "We'll miss you."

"Later," he answers, without stopping.

He is about to clear the threshold, to find his freedom from class, when I call him back momentarily. "Oh, Matt," I say. "Happy birthday."

He shakes the hair from his eyes again. "Touché," he answers. And then he is gone. And everyone remaining in the classroom—all twenty-nine of my senior composition students—is staring at me with the same look prisoners must give the prison warden when one among their number has, inexplicably, escaped.

"What?" I say to them.

"Can he *do* that?" someone answers.

"Of course he can. He absolutely can. He's eighteen—remember? The law gives him permission to leave on his own authority, for his own reasons, for any reason. He's an adult now. He can do as he pleases."

"But so are you," says another voice. "Could you, like, leave too, if you wanted? I mean, I don't *get* this. He can *leave*?"

"He can, but I can't—at least not without violating my contract. Sure I could leave, but I wouldn't get paid and chances are, if I did it more than once, I'd lose my job. So the answer is no, I can't leave. I can't leave, not because the law says I can't—there's no law saying I can't quit my job—but because leaving entails consequences I can't accept and, furthermore, don't want. Now what about Matt? Are there consequences?"

We talk about what Matt might miss by not being with us—the learning, the social interaction, the push and pull, the give and take—then Sara Earlheimer, precocious and bold, points out that my children, because they are homeschooled, are missing out on all those things, on all the advantages of school attendance I've elicited, she says, under the pretense of guiding a discussion. "If school's so wonderful," she finishes, "how come your children don't go to it?"

"We've already talked about that," I tell her. "We've been all up and down homeschooling." (It was the first thing my students had wanted to discuss: Word had got around.) "But you know what? Before Matt acted on his rights as an adult we were on the subject of supporting evidence for thesis statements. I don't mind digressing from that for a while but—"

"But how come it's even legal?" asks Sara Earlheimer. "How come we all sort of *have* to be here, and if we're not, it's like skipping, and like your kids don't even—is it even *legal*?"

I tell Sara that if she persists in discussing it I will be forced to do the teacherly thing and twist matters back toward the curriculum. This is school, I remind her. There's a subject at hand designated by a committee of educators who did not take into account her impulse or desire to focus on something else.

"Should homeschooling be legal?" I say to the class. "All right, let's pretend it's an essay question. Let's pretend you have to compose a thesis about it. Does anybody want to take a stab, here, at composing a thesis statement? One you believe in? That you feel you can support? Anybody?"

Hands go up, and for the next twenty minutes we try out a variety of positions on homeschooling: It should be legal; it shouldn't be legal; it should be legal under certain conditions, with certain restrictions, with certain guidelines, within certain boundaries. My students articulate a number of good ideas and seem enthusiastic about the subject. Nevertheless, there is a chorus of disbelieving gasps and groans when, near the end of the period, I announce an essay assignment. "Thousand-word minimum," I tell them as the bell rings. "A clear thesis and strong support. Should homeschooling be legal? That's your question."

"Maybe, maybe not," answers one boy. "But thousand-word papers definitely shouldn't be legal. They're, like, a felony. You should get twenty years for assigning one."

"Life," says another boy. "Life at least. Maybe the electric chair."

"Write about that instead," I reply. "Why thousand-word essays should be illegal."

"Great," somebody else says on his way out of the room. "Wait'll I tell Brush what he got us into. If it wasn't for that dink we—"

"Brush," interrupts his neighbor. "Oh, yeah, right, Brush. You'll find him in the library reading *War and Peace*. He's—"

"Yeah, *right*," his neighbor shoots back. "By now he's crashed on his couch. He's watching TV and eating Cheetos. He's tuned into MTV."

"*Crime and Punishment.* The library."

"The Brady Bunch." "Star Trek." "The Flintstones."

"No way. *Dante's Inferno. Pride and Prejudice. Moby Dick. The* . . ."

Then they are gone from the room. I erase all traces of homeschooling from the blackboard. I would not want my coming ninth graders to catch wind of this. We would never get to *Romeo and Juliet.*

In order for my composition students to decide where they stand, they will need to know far more than they currently do. That is the first lesson about thesis statements, I tell them: You can't devise one until you know your subject.

For the purpose of acquainting them with homeschooling law I draw on the expertise of a guest speaker, a willing and able Seattle criminal attorney who has represented the interests of homeschoolers in the courts: namely my father, Murray Guterson, a man who has always been philosophically opposed to homeschooling but who nevertheless supports my right to practice it.

So on a wet afternoon in mid-April he stands before my senior composition students and tells them, first, that if ever I chide them for not minding me, just remember that when your teacher was a boy, he didn't always mind his elders either. The wording of this opener is so charmingly archaic that none of them quite knows what to make of my father; but then, so much about him is charmingly archaic. He is a big, rumpled, gray man from a past era in history (just after the dull suits of the Eisenhower cabinet but easily before the paisley tie came along), a man whose shirts are loudly unfashionable, who has always worn both sideburns and suspenders, a pen in his shirt pocket, and a polite, attentive expression. He slides black glasses up his nose to read notes, then removes them and clamps their right stem between his teeth: My father is forever either gesturing with these glasses or removing them fumblingly from his jacket pocket, putting them away or putting them on, chewing them or folding their stems closed. At sixty-two he is poised between near- and farsightedness, can't see with glasses and can't see without them, is neither young anymore nor really old—though to my students he is certainly an old man. His thinning hair is gray, his suit loose fitting, yet there is nevertheless something impressive in him that elicits an attentive silence. I like to think this something is his eyes, which are simultaneously benign and intense.

"I've never done anything but criminal work," he tells them. "Before that I sold shoes. If the law were just contracts and companies suing each other, I'd still be selling shoes today. Fortunately, though, I went to law school. In fifty-nine I tried my first homeschooling case, and since then I've tried a dozen others, and I've found them all to be interesting. Seems to me you've got to understand the basic principles behind these kinds of cases before you try writing your papers. So that's what we're going to do today: talk principles, legal principles."

He finds a piece of chalk in the blackboard tray, then slides his glasses into place so that suddenly he looks five years older. "The laws about homeschooling are like a lot of other laws in that they operate at different levels," he says. "At the lowest level are regulations"—in his tight, legal hand he writes *regulations* on the board, rapidly, his chalk clacking loudly against the slate—"which are enacted by a state's department of education. That means that somebody in an Olympia office building is authorized by our legislators to write codes governing education. For example, that the school year will last one hundred and eighty days or that the school day will last six hours. That you will study English and social studies but not Chinese or basket weaving. Those sorts of things, you see, are regulations, and they have the force of law; that is, citizens are bound by them. So the first question in a homeschooling case is, What state regulations govern homeschooling, and have the homeschoolers who have been called to court in fact failed to live up to those regulations? For example, supposing the regulations codified by the state of Washington called for all homeschooling parents to be certified teachers. Supposing that were a regulation. If it were and the homeschooling parent failed to get himself certified, then clearly he would be violating a state regulation, and at that point he might need a lawyer.

"Now," says my father, "the lawyer can go into the courtroom and argue, 'Hey, my client is certified. Look, here's his certificate.' But if it turns out his client isn't certified, he'll have to drum up another argument, otherwise his client is going to be found guilty of violating the state's regulation. So what can the lawyer do? What does he do next? He takes a close look at the regulation itself and sees if *it* violates something—let's say the next level of law, state statutes, which are more powerful than any regulation. If the regulation contradicts a statute or if it isn't authorized by a statute, then it may be that the regulation won't hold up to scrutiny, and your client no longer has a problem."

Just beneath the word *regulations* my father writes *state statutes*. "Any questions so far?" he asks the class. "Anything you're confused about?"

He waits for a moment, scans faces. My students all look intimidated. My father is a manic, high-speed speaker when the details of his subject move him. He is so earnest, lively, and enthusiastic, it would be a crime, they must feel, to question him: They'd be getting, somehow, in the way.

"Okay," says my father, "so just above the level of state regulations are these things I'm now calling statutes. These are the laws you're probably most familiar with, the ones enacted by legislators and signed into law by governors. These have to do with how much you'll pay in state sales tax or how fast you'll drive on the state's roads or whether or not you'll have to wear a helmet when you ride a motorcycle—most of the laws you know about are in this category of the state statute. For example, Washington State has a Home School Statute that says, among other things, that any parent who decides to homeschool must meet one and only one of five conditions. He must be a certified teacher; or two, be supervised by a certified teacher an hour a week; or three, have under his belt one year of college; or four, complete a homeschool training course; or five, convince his local superintendent he's qualified to homeschool. This is statute, that he must meet one of these five conditions, and any regulation that required, say, *two* of these things from a homeschooling parent would directly contradict it. In such a case the regulation would be superseded by the higher level of statute law, and the regulation would be declared by a court null and void. Your client would go home trouble-free.

"But," says my father, "supposing a regulation is consistent with state statute? Supposing an attorney can't argue in court that a regulation contradicts a statute passed by the legislature and signed into law by the governor? Is he dead in the water? Not quite. Not yet. He can turn his attention to a third level of law, a level even higher than the statutes I've been talking about. These are court decisions interpreting these statutes, generally in light of the constitution, be it our state constitution or our federal one."

Beneath *state statutes* my father writes *court decisions*. He has already begun to tire, I notice; his tenor voice sounds a little stretched, his forehead is flushed a pale pink. My father, from his own point of view, has been perfectly clear about everything; he has repeated himself often out of the lawyer's hope that he will not be misunderstood. On the other hand he has no sympathy for those who lose concentration in the midst of his orderly progressions. I look out over my composition students. He has so far lost only three or four.

"All right," he says. "The supreme law of this state is our state constitution, but the supreme law of the land—the whole United States—is our national Constitution, the one you learned about in civics class. It is a magnificent document. As much as this country believes in states' rights and in the rights of states to make their own laws, no state can pass a law that violates the Constitution. So judges are constantly hearing cases that turn on whether or not a state statute is constitutional, and this means that they are constantly in the business of interpreting statutes, state constitutions, and the federal Constitution. Now, let's suppose, hypothetically, that a state has a homeschooling statute requiring that every homeschooling program contain a specific religious element based on, say, Christian precepts. In other words, that if you homeschool your child, you have to teach him the Christian Bible. Would a judge have a problem—a constitutional problem—with a statute of that nature? Yes?"

Sara Earlheimer mentions the First Amendment, the clause having to do with separation of church and state, and my father nods vigorously. "You're a hundred percent right," he says to her. "A judge is going to find a statute of that sort in violation of the First Amendment. Government cannot be in the business of requiring families to provide their children with a specific sort of religious instruction. A statute of that sort wouldn't hold up for one moment under court scrutiny.

"Okay," he says. "I hope you can see how this third level of law—court interpretations of statutes and constitutions—would supersede the very statutes themselves and the even lower level of state regulation. But be careful. Court decisions don't have the force of law and generally act only as precedents that guide courts when hearing subsequent cases. If you actually want to change the regulations or statutes instead of merely having grounds for challenging them during the course of a particular case, you're going to have to go to our state constitution or beyond that to the highest level of law in this country—our national Constitution itself."

My father writes on the board again. His list now looks like this:

> regulations
> state statutes
> court decisions
> state constitutions
> federal Constitution

"Well," he says. "The federal Constitution. A regulation, a state statute, a court decision, the state constitution—the federal Constitution supersedes all of these. So the question—the real question—for homeschooling families is what the federal Constitution says about what they're doing. But," my father says, his glasses in hand again, the chalk back in its tray, "the Constitution never mentions homeschooling; at best it merely implies its protection under several different amendments. In fact, the Constitution never even mentions education, at least not in the Bill of Rights, which is the section we're talking about. For a document so significant to just about everything in this country it is strangely silent on so important a matter; but never mind that—there's nothing about homeschooling. There's nothing plain and simple in the Constitution about whether a person has the right to homeschool.

"You can ask your history teacher about this one, he or she would know best, but from what I understand the Constitution doesn't mention homeschooling in part because its writers didn't have the word in their vocabulary. Learning outside of schools, back then, was pretty common. Benjamin Franklin, for example, didn't go to school. In the past, governments didn't take it upon themselves to see to education. They didn't think of it as their proper role as governments do today.

"Anyway," my father says, "the Constitution is silent on homeschooling. It is, however, loud and clear about other things that the courts have seen as related. It is loud and clear about the rights of parents and about the rights of citizens to practice their religion. The First Amendment, as you know from civics, protects your right to worship as you see fit. The Fourteenth grants certain rights to parents under something called the due-process clause. Then you've got other, less obvious aspects of the Constitution that turn out to be meaningful in homeschooling cases. Take the Ninth Amendment, which says that 'The enumeration in the Constitution of certain basic rights shall not be construed to deny or disparage others retained by the people.' This means, to name just one thing, that you can travel freely from state to state even though the Constitution doesn't spell that out specifically as a right. It means you don't automatically lose a right just because the Constitution doesn't mention it. An amendment like that gives courts a lot of room. It's an all-purpose amendment, don't you think? If a right doesn't fit in anywhere else, a lawyer can try to claim it's a right retained by the people under the Ninth Amendment, okay?

"Go back even further than the Constitution. Go back to the seventeen hundreds and read Sir William Blackstone. Go back to cases tried in the last century. What you're going to find wherever you look is that lawyers and courts have recognized parental rights as fundamental, as so fundamental and so obvious that they need no specific enumeration but are simply taken for granted. Parents have the right to direct their children's education, and this right is superior, in a basic way, to the interests of the state—not always, but in a basic way, mind you; not in every case, but as a fundamental principle. If you live in a democracy and if you want to take responsibility for educating your children, the fundamental principle is that you should be allowed to. For the state to intervene would be anathema to what a free nation is all about, don't you think? Certainly it would be.

"But," says my father, "the rights of individuals and the interests of the state clash anyway, all the time, and the conflict between them is worked out in courtrooms. Now, the first clash that has any significant bearing on your essay assignment is a case called *Pierce v. Society of Sisters*, heard in the Supreme Court in 1925, four years before I was born." My father writes *Pierce v. Society of Sisters—1925* on the left side of the blackboard, then stands with his stub of chalk in one hand and his glasses between the fingers of the other. "In *Pierce*," he says, "the Court overturned an Oregon state statute requiring public-school education. It did so by pointing out that the interest of the state in seeing to the education of all its children was not powerful enough to overcome the basic right of parents to control their own child's education. I've got a good quote from the

Court," he says, "up here"—my father taps his forefinger against his forehead—"if I can remember it correctly."

But, of course, he remembers it perfectly. " 'The fundamental theory of liberty,' " he says, " 'upon which all governments in this Union repose excludes any general power of the State to standardize its children by forcing them to accept instruction from public school teachers only. The child is not the mere creature of the State; those who nurture and direct his destiny have the right, coupled with the high duty, to recognize and prepare him for additional obligations.'

"So in *Pierce*," says my father, "the Court establishes this principle: that parents have a right to control their child's education. It did so again just two years later in *Farrington v. Tokushige*." My father writes *Farrington v. Tokushige*—1927 beneath *Pierce*, then drops his chalk in the tray again. "I need my notes for this," he explains, slides his glasses on, then takes up the yellow legal pad he's perched on the corner of my desk. "In *Farrington* the Court wrote that 'a parent has the right to direct the education of his own child without unreasonable restriction.' So twice in two years, in nineteen twenty-five and twenty-seven the high court reiterated the basic point that parents have a right to control and direct their own child's education. And that's not to mention yet another case, *Meyer v. Nebraska*, which made a similar point as far back as nineteen twenty-three. But how many cases can I throw at you?"

My father turns again to the blackboard, takes up his chalk, and writes beneath *Farrington* the words *Meyer v. Nebraska*—1923, then *Wisconsin v. Yoder*—1972.

"This one—*Yoder*—I was around for," he tells the class. "Even your teacher was around for this one. In nineteen seventy-two he was a high-school soph-o-more, younger than you are now.

"*Wisconsin v. Yoder*," he says, without looking at me. "*Wisconsin v. Yoder* is, in its own way, probably the most important Supreme Court decision for anybody who homeschools. Not only did it reiterate less than twenty years ago the precedent set in *Pierce* and *Farrington*—the one about parental control over a child's education—it also changed the nature of the whole ball game by bringing in the First Amendment and making the free exercise of religion an issue. The Yoders, you see, were an Amish family who didn't want to send their child to a public high school; they felt that Wisconsin's compulsory attendance law asked them—forced them—to abandon their *religious* belief in *religious* home training. In this case the Supreme Court held that the Yoders' First Amendment right to the free exercise of their religion overcame the state's interest in mandating that every child attend school. So the Yoders won on two premises, and it turns out there are two powerful constitutional principles that protect the rights of homeschooling families: One is the right of parents to direct the education of their children, as in *Pierce*; the other is the right of all Americans—Amish, Methodists, Baptists, Buddhists, Jews, *everybody*—to the free exercise of their religion. *Yoder* turns on both these principles. In that regard it is a landmark case."

A hand goes up. It is Matthew Brush in the back row, rising up, stirred out of his habitual sulk; he is in class because even ten *excused* absences provide grounds for a failing grade. My father points at him and says, "Yes, sir. In the back."

"Okay," says Matthew. "Supposing someone *pretends* to be religious? Like, says they're religious even though they aren't? And also, what if you don't go to a church but just sort of have your own ideas about . . . God and everything? Like, you're not *officially* religious?"

"Excellent," my father answers. "Two excellent questions.

The answer—let's take number one first—is that you can't pretend to be religious because in cases that turn on whether or not the homeschooling family is acting on sincere religious beliefs the court will demand the family prove that its belief is indeed genuine. The family will have to show that it must homeschool because its faith directs it to. It will have to point to, say, Biblical passages that direct parents to teach their young or passages from the Koran, to name another equally valid source in the eyes of the law. Okay? Is that clear? Number two, the law is fundamentally clear about religious motivations for choosing homeschooling: So long as a homeschooling family defines its motivation as religious—whether that religion be Catholicism or Hinduism or some new, modern faith not widely recognized and practiced only by a very few—so long as the homeschooling family convincingly characterizes its motivation as religious it will be protected by the free-exercise clause of the First Amendment. All right? Okay? Even if no other Catholics do it, even if there are Catholic schools, even if everybody else in your parish sends their children to school, even then, if you feel your being a Catholic requires that you homeschool, well then, the court must respect this. It's your right, after all, as a citizen.

"Sometimes, though," my father pushes on, "the state has a legitimate compelling interest that overcomes the rights of citizens. It can declare a curfew or even martial law if it feels that in so doing a compelling interest is served, and the curfew will stand up to a challenge in court from a citizen who feels his rights are being violated. 'You can't be on the street after midnight,' the judge will say, 'because there is a compelling state interest, like public safety, in keeping everybody off, including you, and that interest overrides your individual right to be on the street at such a time.' Now, the same principle can be applied to homeschooling. The state can argue that it has a compelling interest in, say, requiring every child between the ages of six and eighteen to be in a school or in seeing that everyone who educates kids has a certificate from its office of education. But," says my father, "the state must demonstrate that this interest is so compelling that it justly overwhelms the right of an individual, and that is not always easy for the state to do, chiefly because judges are big on the Constitution and do not lightly allow governments to deny Americans their fundamental, constitutional rights."

My father stops to catch his breath. He perches himself on the edge of my desk and slides his glasses on.

"Another problem for the state," he says, hands in his lap, shoulders hunched. "Not only must it demonstrate that this compelling interest is so overwhelmingly compelling that it's more important than a person's constitutional rights, but it— the state—must also show that it has used what lawyers call *the least restrictive means* of achieving that interest. Take, for example, the state's interest in seeing all children educated. In order for the state to force a homeschooler to go to school it will have to show first that homeschooling doesn't serve this interest and second that the thing serving it least restrictively is mandatory school attendance. The state must show that it has used the least restrictive means—not just any old means at hand, like legally preventing a person from homeschooling—to achieve its compelling interest.

"Incidentally," says my father, "even a guy like me—a guy who doesn't think homeschooling is a good thing—even a guy like me has to say that academically, at least, homeschooling works. The evidence is pretty much overwhelming, and most judges would be impressed by it. So no state counsel in his right mind would go to court arguing that a compelling state interest in education is served by a statute making homeschooling illegal. If anything, you could argue that in a lot of cases schools *prevent* the state from seeing its compelling interest served. The failure rate of schools—your teacher likes to point this out—is a serious threat to the state's interest in seeing all children educated."

He rises, removes his glasses, folds their stems, slips them into his coat pocket. "Well," he says, "so far I've been talking about big principles. In the real world, though—the real world of the courtroom—cases turn on little nuances, subtle things you wouldn't normally think about but that make good sense when you consider them. Every state, after all, has a different set of rules regarding home education. It isn't simple, and the big principles of *Pierce* and *Yoder* and compelling interest and least restrictive means aren't always the important points.

"Even with the Constitution," he points out, "some things are bigger than others. The First Amendment protection of the free exercise of religion is pretty big, as I've said; so is the Fourteenth Amendment's protection of parental privilege inherent in the due-process clause. But take the Ninth for a minute, that all-purpose amendment I touched on earlier, a more subtle and ambiguous amendment. The Supreme Court of this land has held in the past that the Ninth implies, among other things, a right to privacy and that this right to privacy includes such matters as child rearing and education." Again he slides his glasses on; again he picks up his yellow legal pad. "Here it is," he says, flipping pages back, "from the presiding judge in *Perchemlides v. Frizzle*: 'The right to privacy, which protects the right to choose alternative forms of education, grows out of constitutional guarantees in addition to those contained in the First Amendment. Nonreligious as well as religious parents have the right to choose from the full range of educational alternatives for their children. There will remain little privacy in the "right to privacy" if the state is permitted to inquire into the motives behind the parents' decision regarding the education of their children.'

"Notice," says my father, "how careful this judge in *Perchemlides* is to point out that nonreligious parents have precisely the same right to homeschool as religious ones. You don't necessarily need the Ninth Amendment to tell you this; you can go back to the First's guarantee of the right to speech, which includes, beneath its umbrella, the rights to freedom of belief and thought." My father turns to the board again, writes *Perchemlides v. Frizzle—1978*, then *In re Falk—1981.* "The Falks wanted to homeschool their children, not because of religious reasons but because they had a philosophical objection to things that happen in public schools. The court viewed this philosophical objection as a belief protected under the umbrella of the First Amendment's free-speech clause. It didn't matter if the Falks were religious or not. They had a philosophical belief they were entitled to under the First Amendment that was equal in the eyes of the law to the religious belief that, say, the Yoders had."

He puts his chalk down, removes his glasses, looks at his watch, turns his eyes to the wall clock. "How much time do we have?" he asks.

"Twenty-one minutes," answers Matt Brush from the back row. "We get out at twelve thirty-five."

"Twelve thirty-five," says my father. "Excellent. Thank you, young man. That's about the time I need to tell you about just a few other things. So far I've been trying to put before you court cases and legal concepts that will help you write your thousand-word essay. You can probably see now you'll have a difficult time arguing for an outright ban on education at home, because you'll keep bumping your nose against different parts of the Constitution—though you might try to make a case that compelling state interests, even when the state seeks them via the least restrictive means, supersede, always, the right to homeschool. You could say, for example, that schools socialize young people in a manner so vital to the state interest and so impossible to achieve elsewhere that the rights of individuals under the First and Ninth and Fourteenth Amendments are less important in the face of it. But how could you make that one fly? It has never flown very well in the courts, so how are you going to do it? No, the essay question your teacher has given you turns not really on whether homeschooling should be legal but, since it must be legal if we take the Constitution seriously, on the question of in what *manner* it should be legal. To what extent should the state regulate it? To what extent should the state control it? What can the state reasonably and fairly ask of those who homeschool without infringing on their constitutional rights?

"Well," says my father, "herein lies a big part of your essay. Different states have tried different things, and you ought to think about which kind of state most fairly regulates the homeschoolers inside its borders before you try to write one paragraph.

"Twenty-eight states," my father presses on, "have statutes about homeschooling. Four others have regulations that, as you know already, are very much different from statutes, though both carry the force of law. So that's thirty-two states altogether that explicitly allow homeschooling. In the other eighteen it's legal, too, but not because of regulations or statutes specific about the practice. In ten of them homeschooling's legal so long as the homeschool is set up as a legal private school; in the remaining eight it's allowed under statutes permitting education 'equivalent' to the public schools'. No matter what state you're talking about, though, you end up running into legal problems.

Nobody seems to know what *equivalent* really means, for example, or a statute will call for a homeschooling parent to be certified as a teacher, and the homeschooling parent will refuse. So there are always these problems of how to regulate homeschooling and this question of the extent to which a state can regulate it before its statutes and regulations become unconstitutionally void.

"Take the matter of parental qualifications," my father says. "Should the state have a right to require homeschooling parents to meet certain minimum qualifications before it allows them to homeschool?"

Hands go up. He points at one and says, "Miss? Young lady?"

"Well, what if the parents can't read or something?" Stacy Bryan asks. "I mean, at least the state should have *some*thing."

"Yes," says my father. "The state should be interested in the qualifications of parents just as it is in the qualifications of teachers—like those, for example, of your English teacher here, who had to go to college and get a degree and a teaching certificate before he could presume to teach you. Should the same thing—a college degree, a certificate—be required of homeschooling parents? The only state requiring homeschooling parents to have a college education is New Mexico, and even in New Mexico there's a way to slip out of it. In some states you only need a high-school diploma; in others you have to pass a teacher-competency test. But in twenty states you don't have to do anything at all as far as qualifications are concerned. All you have to do is be ready and willing. You don't need anything but willingness.

"The interesting thing," my father points out, "is this series of studies here in Washington State that show that the level of parent education doesn't matter. College degree, high-school degree, master's degree, Ph.D.—the kids of parents with all these different qualifications do equally well on standardized achievement tests. You can't tell the kids apart—not by the qualifications of their parents. Even somebody like me, who really thinks deep down inside that homeschooling is just absolutely wrong-headed, even a guy like me has to see that, if you look at the test results, parental education is a moot point, it's absolutely superfluous. And look here, what about subjects and courses of study for homeschoolers and the number of hours they should actively homeschool? Do you think the state ought to regulate those things? Most states do—in fact, almost all of them. But should they? And what about forcing homeschooling parents to notify the authorities of their intent to homeschool? Should they have to? And should their kids have to take tests every year or so to demonstrate that they're getting along just fine? Let's take the testing question. What do you think?"

"*We* have to take tests," says one student. "It's only fair they should too."

"Yes," says my father. "But you don't have to pass a standardized test before you can pass from one grade to the next, do you? So should homeschoolers have to pass one before they're allowed to go on homeschooling? If you fail a standardized test, my friend, are you forced to drop out of school? And if a homeschooled child fails one, should he be forced to stop homeschooling? And what about this?" asks my father. "I would guess that, oh, a couple of times a year a principal or a vice principal comes into this room to see how your English teacher is getting along and to evaluate his performance, to see if he is doing the job he's supposed to do and to figure out how well he's doing it. So supposing a state-education official wants to walk into a homeschooler's home and look at what's going on for the same reasons. Shouldn't the state have the right to inspect the homeschool the same way it inspects this class-room?"

"They'd have to have a search warrant," says Matthew Brush. "No way can they just come in."

"They can in North Carolina," says my father, "and in South Dakota too. But you're right, sir, in the vast majority of states such a home visit would be seen as an invasion of privacy and as an intrusion on the part of government. Another tough, tough matter," says my father. "Something else for you to contemplate.

"Or how about this?" he asks next. He writes *home visits* on the blackboard, then *child neglect and abuse*. "What if the parents are accused of neglecting the child or of abusing him by keeping him at home? What if they aren't really seeing to the child's education but instead are letting him do whatever he wants for most hours of the day, watch television and eat cupcakes? Or making him sit in the cellar all day? Should the state force them to send the child to school? If so, can we also argue that the failures of schoolchildren constitute neglect or abuse on the part of schoolteachers or administrators or the state itself? Certainly the failure rate among schoolchildren is far higher than among homeschoolers. If *failure to educate* means child neglect or even child abuse, well then, I'll tell you what, plenty of our schools are in big trouble—and I'm a guy who stands one hundred percent behind the public schools, mind you. I'm a guy who thinks they're swell, flawed maybe, but central to what America is all about."

My father rests on the edge of the desk again. He checks his watch. He sighs.

"Okay," he says. "Just a couple more things then before the bell. I wouldn't want to keep you even one extra minute. So I'll move rapidly here. I want you to think next about these eight states I've mentioned that have equivalency laws. These are laws that say you can homeschool so long as what you do is equivalent to what schools do. But look here for a moment. How can any homeschooling family do exactly what a school does? How can it provide a child with the same kind of social opportunity, for example? It can't, you see; it just can't. So does that mean there's no such thing as a homeschool that is equivalent to a public school? Lawyers have tried to argue that; they've tried to say, in these eight states, that homeschooling is made impossible by statutes requiring equivalency. In the *Perchemlides* case I mentioned earlier the presiding judge wrote that 'there are certain ways in which individualized home instruction can never be the "equivalent" of any in-school education, private or public. . . . [To] require congruent "equivalency" is self-defeating because it might foreclose the use of teaching methods less formalized, but in the home more effective than those in the classroom.' " My father pulls his glasses from his face, folds them, and puts them away. "*Perchemlides* ruled out even socialization as a basis for compelling school attendance," he says. "It's a very important case.

"Something else," he tells the class. "What about states requiring teacher certification? Recall that I mentioned before some studies that showed how the education of parents didn't matter one iota when you looked at homeschoolers' test scores. The same can be said for certification, you see. Not one iota of difference. Whether the parent has a certificate or not has no bearing on the test scores of children. So why should states require certificates? Are certificates an unreasonable burden to place on homeschooling parents? Do certificates guarantee that, at least academically, the homeschool will be 'equivalent' to the public school? There have been some good cases in this area. *Iowa v. Sessions*, for example, provides for what you might call a general assumption of competence on the part of parents, a lot like the general assumption of innocence on the part of the accused that holds in criminal proceedings. In other words, certificate or no, homeschooling parents are assumed capable of teaching their children unless the state proves otherwise. A couple of other important cases—*Hinton v. Kentucky Board of Education, Michigan v. Nobel*—support the basic idea of *Sessions*: They all say that instructional competence is not necessarily a function of certification, which is just a fancy way of saying that in these cases it was made pretty clear that homeschooling parents don't necessarily need certificates to teach well."

My father, chalk in hand, writes *Iowa v. Sessions—1978, Hinton v. Kentucky Board of Education—1978*, and *Michigan v. Nobel—1979*. Then once again he slides his black glasses into place and takes up his yellow legal pad.

"That's pretty straightforward," he points out, "but judges haven't always agreed. Just three years ago, in *People of Michigan v. DeJonge*, a court found that though the burden of the certification requirement was large, the state nevertheless had a compelling interest in the education of its children and that requiring certification was the least restrictive means of serving it. Remember those terms? *Least restrictive means* and *compelling state interest*. You see what a difference they can make?

"The fact of the matter is," says my father, "that the courts have gone both ways on homeschooling. It's still all up in the air on every count. You still get every kind of decision, favorable and unfavorable to homeschoolers. So sooner or later the Supreme Court's going to have to say something absolutely definitive about education at home, or the legal cases will go on forever. With so many people, like your teacher over here, deciding they want to teach their own children, it's getting to be a social issue of the kind the Supreme Court can't neglect. But look, that's neither here nor there. Maybe with just a couple of minutes left I ought to take any questions."

He stands there peering over his glasses at me. From my perch by the windows he looks stooped and old, scraggly eye-browed, a little disheveled. Behind him the blackboard is covered with legal scrawlings. He turns to look at it, sees something like this:

Pierce v. Society of Sisters—*1925* regulations parental qualifications

Farrington v. Tokushige—*1927* state statutes courses of study

Meyer v. Nebraska—*1923* court decisions number of hours

Wisconsin v. Yoder—*1972* state constitutions notifying authorities

Perchemlides v. Frizzle—*1978* federal Constitution

In re Falk—*1981* testing

Iowa v. Sessions—*1978* home visits

Hinton v. Kentucky Board of Education—*1978*

Michigan v. Nobel—*1979* child neglect and abuse

My father picks up his chalk and adds:

> certification
> equivalency
> compelling state interest
> least restrictive means

"I can't do everything," he says.

"Question," says Sara Earlheimer, her hand in the air. My father calls on her, calls her Miss, which provokes from Sara an embarrassed laugh. "Okay," she says. "You said before you thought homeschooling was bad. That you're against it? First, I kind of wanted to know why you're against it; second, I wanted to know, if you're against it, how come you help homeschoolers in court cases? So it's two questions, I guess."

"Two questions," says my father. "Two excellent questions. All right: I'm against homeschooling for reasons I don't really have time to go into, but basically because I think kids who are schooled at home are going to miss out on some absolutely essential formative experiences. They're not ever going to sit in a classroom and have the joy of getting an answer right, say, or the embarrassment of getting an answer wrong; they're not going to have to sit through a class that's boring or dry or mundane, and they're not going to have the chance to meet a Mr. Guterson with all the things he has to say about books and writing and poetry. They're just missing an experience that's absolutely fundamental, that's all I can say for now. But—to answer your second question—while I might feel this way, it doesn't for one second prevent me from recognizing that people like your teacher, people who want to teach their children at home, have a perfectly legal right to do so, and as a lawyer it's my job to protect that right and to represent their interest when it's challenged. I might be against homeschooling in my heart, but I would never want to see laws entirely against it. It's a right I wish people wouldn't exercise, but it's a right, and they're entitled to do it. Yes, young man," my father says, pointing at Matthew Brush. "There's time for one more question."

But the bell rings just then, and my students, being who they are, begin their movement toward the door. I ask them to take a moment to thank my father for coming in this day, and this elicits from them a smattering of applause. Only Matthew Brush stays behind for a moment. "I think it should be illegal," he tells my father. "There's too many crazy, off-the-wall people in this country, like these people who start little cults and every-thing, and homeschooling gives them the right to just, like, totally brainwash their kids. And then we'll have a whole bunch of people running around who never went to school and . . . I don't know . . . the government just shouldn't let them because otherwise, everything will fall apart."

"Well," says my father, packing his briefcase, "there's two sides to it, just as you say, my friend. It's true that when you give people rights, some of them will abuse those rights or use them irresponsibly. They'll act selfishly or stupidly, and they'll do things you and I might disagree with. And I guess one answer is just to take rights away because certain individuals abuse them. Take freedom of speech away because some people use it to advocate murdering blacks and Jews. Take freedom of religion away because people who worship the devil claim protection from it. You see what I mean? There are a lot of frightening people in this country, and if this were a dictatorship, they might not be protected by a document like the Constitution. But, thank God, we're not a dictatorship. We have certain rights, and even though some individuals abuse them, let's just be thankful they're there, all right?"

"Like the attendance rights of eighteen-year-olds," I tell Matthew Brush. "Certain students in this school might abuse those rights. Does that mean—"

"I get the picture, okay?" Matthew Brush says. "You don't have to rub it in."

Three weeks later I bring my father copies of twenty-four student papers. Six students—par for the course—simply did not do the assignment. Four wrote merely a single page. Eleven wrote two pages. Only the remaining nine met the minimum-length requirement for the essay. Of those, most had no identifiable thesis or made few references to facts or arguments that might, indeed, support a thesis. Three were thought provoking.

(Again, this is par for the course at a high school with an excellent academic reputation.) One—Sara Earlheimer's—made the case that homeschooling should be legal within certain strict boundaries of state control and regulation; a second—Matthew Brush's—called for its outright ban on the grounds of compelling state interest. The best among them was by a girl named Jamie Browning, a quiet student whose writing I had admired all semester, who argued that laws preventing homeschooling were fundamentally unconstitutional but that the state's interest in seeing all children educated was nevertheless important and that in the conflict between them the most refined, sophisticated, and intelligent laws would emerge. Her balanced approach was duly noted by my father, who sent me a letter about it in his crimped hand and, as always, on yellow legal paper. "She's right," he said. "Nothing is black and white, nothing is simple, nothing all good or all bad. There are two sides to everything, homeschooling included. I admit to that and always will. Now do the right thing and send my grandchildren to school, will you? It's getting awfully late."

5

School, Home, and History

It is not difficult to imagine a boy of the Mbuti people, in Zaire, rising in the morning when his father does and following his father's path into the forest. It is more difficult to imagine the son of my neighbor commuting each morning alongside his father to the downtown offices of SeaFirst Bank. To put it another way, our culture is for children vague and abstract, whereas in "primitive" societies culture was visible and easily in reach, and children learned much of what they needed to know by sharing in what their elders were doing and playing games in imitation of them. Certain matters—the crafting of a water jug, for instance, the weaving of a cedar-bark hat, a curing ritual or medicinal practice—were best transmitted by deliberate training, but much education went forward without calling attention to itself as a process distinct from life. The young, as Margaret Mead has noted, fully participated in the social life of the community and, having come to identify with the activities of adults, naturally took to adult roles. In many past cultures one's only formal education came at the verge of adolescence, its purpose not so much practical as spiritual, part of a young person's initiation into the mysteries of the adult world. The idea was to uproot him at age twelve or so from the secure haven of his family and to establish—via an immersion in tribal religion, lore, myth, philosophy, history, and ritual—his place in the larger society.

As societies grew more complex, however, they began to create formal schools. It no longer seemed possible—in ancient Egypt, to cite one example—for everyone to learn what they needed to know mostly by observing and imitating. Egyptian agriculture required scribes, and Egyptian architecture mathematicians. There could be no pyramids without engineers steeped in the useful abstractions of geometry. The result was schools as places of learning and teachers as specialists in education. (Egyptian teachers, incidentally, were priests, and Egyptian students were exclusively males of the upper class. Schooling began at age five and concluded at seventeen, with training for the priesthood taking longer.) The details, of course, differed from culture to culture, but every significant early civilization—the Mesopotamians, the Chinese, the Mayans, the Incas, the Aztecs, and others—established formal systems of education in response to increasing social complexity.

These new systems of education spawned peculiar new difficulties. The inherent rigidity of schooling posed a problem because it cut against the grain of children who were not naturally predisposed to long hours of physical inactivity or to rigorous and disciplined intellectual work far removed from what they valued. In Europe, at least, by the eighteenth century, schools had become relatively joyless places where an education almost entirely divorced from daily life went relentlessly forward. Culture itself, with its enormous complexity—its government officials and systems of taxation, its accountants and libraries and sailing ships—was by this time increasingly made up of abstractions, and to discover it fully and ultimately internalize it children—the argument went—had to be rigorously schooled.

In eighteenth-century Europe this inherent rigor gained sustenance from other potent forces: a monastic tradition of scholarly diligence, the Enlightenment emphasis on the systematic pursuit of knowledge, the new Protestant work ethic. Education in Europe became increasingly regimented: In German Pietist schools children studied twelve to fourteen hours a day under extraordinarily close supervision; instruction was virtually continuous, and no games or recesses were permitted. A field trip taken to observe factory work was viewed as recreation, as were lathe work and glass polishing. Schools, in short, battled the child's innate sinfulness and purged him of his willful depravity; they were rigorous because the human spirit was corrupt and demanded rigor if it was to be subdued.

The most significant response to highly regimented schools came from the philosopher Jean-Jacques Rousseau, who in the mid-eighteenth century started a revolution in educational theory that broadly influenced educational thought thereafter in the Western world. Rousseau insisted that children were—contrary to the Christian doctrine of original sin—good in the most basic sense of the word; the job of educators was to help them develop "naturally" or in accordance with their "natures." Rousseau's educational treatise *Emile* espoused limited academic work prior to age twelve and plenty of physical activity, play, and games for children out-of-doors. Young people, the book suggested, should pursue their education in the world of nature and not in texts or schools. Only after age fifteen does Emile, the book's hero, begin to pursue academic training in ethics, religion, and history. Even then, the bulk of his learning arises out of his experiences in the world.

According to Rousseau, a child should be educated not merely for future employment but as a human being, with senses fully alive and independence of thought fully developed, with nature as the ground of his learning and his education gently cultivated by thoughtful and sensitive adults. The notion is one to which, more than two centuries later, many homeschoolers still subscribe.

Emile appeared in 1762—two years before James Watt devised his steam engine and fourteen years before the United States declared its independence. Meanwhile, more than a hundred years earlier, the New England Puritans had established town schools and the Commonwealth of Massachusetts had enacted legislation requiring its towns to hire teachers. The Commonwealth instituted a system of Latin schools that operated according to two novel ideas: that students should be compelled by law to attend and that parents should be compelled by law to pay taxes in support of these mandatory schools, the first of their kind in the modern world. These radical notions gained little currency among common people; most families evaded both the tax and attendance laws, and mandatory, state-supported schooling seemed to them a clear imposition on the part of government.

Furthermore the Latin schools, a creation of the Puritans and of the seventeenth century, were out of step with the times within a hundred years. Their emphasis on languages no longer much used—Latin and Greek, even ancient Hebrew—and on reading classical literature in the original was at odds with a mercantile, colonial economy creating opportunity for those well versed in practical matters: navigation, geography, mathematics, applied science, chronology, modern languages, and the like. A child with these subjects under his belt could get along in the New World, even flourish there, as long as his learning was *useful*, as Ben Franklin described it. This need for "useful learning" inspired the creation of private schools—Franklin's Philadelphia Academy was first in 1751, eleven years before *Emile*—academies dedicated to educating the rich in those subjects required to keep them rich in a world ruled by trade.

At the time of the American Revolution, however, it was still true that most New World children did not attend schools of any sort. The drive toward state-sponsored, compulsory education had been met by a general antagonism. Most children—among them such early presidents as George Washington, James Madison, and John Quincy Adams—received the bulk of their education at home, the wealthy often from private tutors, others from extended families and apprenticeships. The method was so successful that the rate of literacy in Massachusetts prior to the advent of compulsory schooling was higher than it would ever be afterward—perhaps as high as 98 percent, it appears. (Immigration, of course, would contribute to changing this as would other factors. Still, we have a far higher percentage of illiterate native English speakers today than we had before compulsory schools took over education.) Parents and communities made educational arrangements that met their particular and local needs, and though later reformers would view these arrangements as inadequate, they produced, for whatever reasons, results superior to our current schools': not only universal literacy but, by one report, basic mathematical facility as well. In fact, if someone had told Americans at the time of the revolution that within a hundred years state-controlled, compulsory schools would be the norm in their new republic, my guess is they would not have believed it. Perhaps, given the tenor of the times, they would have held out hope that the new freedom meant something else entirely.

But state-controlled schools did develop, and they have their roots in the common-school crusade, which began in earnest during the 1820s. The notion of the common school was quint-essentially American as well as a logical product of the Enlightenment: a free education, tax supported, as the birthright of every citizen. It is no coincidence that it germinated with Jacksonian Democrats who envisioned schools as "an agency for eliminating all privilege and destroying all elites by giving all men the same good 'common' education: 'common' as in common to all, not as in lowest common denominator."

The common-school crusaders were believers in an ideal Jefferson had promoted unsuccessfully at the birth of the nation; namely, education at public cost as an effective instrument of democracy. They called for the establishment of free public schools that would be both compulsory and universal, and they did so, most historians say, in the spirit of egalitarianism. Revisionist historians, on the other hand, see them as promoting the new schools not chiefly out of democratic zeal but to protect their class advantage; the aim of the movement was to provide trained, compliant workers to the new industrial society. Whatever their motives, exploitive or humanitarian—and whichever analysis we choose to take seriously—the common-school crusaders met resistance from every quarter. The wealthy did not want to pay for the schooling of the poor, the churches did not want to give up their crucial role in education, and the average American still believed what only a minority believe today: that education is by right a family matter first and not properly dictated by government.

The principle of state authority over education took half a century to establish. In 1837 Massachusetts convened a state board of education, with Horace Mann—the guiding light of the common-school movement—as its secretary. Two years later the first common school opened in Lexington; within a decade there were three in Massachusetts and financial support for the idea had doubled. The wealthy were slowly coming around to the proposition: Those who understood the common-school concept recognized its economic value. The churches were defeated only after a bitter fight with Mann, who recommended the Scriptures for use in the schools as a guide to moral values exclusively and not as the source of all truth. Meanwhile the common people mostly refused to attend common schools, sometimes resisting, by one report, with guns: The citizens of Barnstable, Massachusetts, held out until the 1880s, when the Commonwealth's militia descended on them and marched their children off to school under guard.

But common people were susceptible to historical forces that made free public schools increasingly acceptable. With industry, men were uprooted from their homes to work in factories, mines, and trade shops; families lost their natural cohesion and with it the will to educate. Housekeeping and child rearing became the province of solitary women for the first time in human history, a condition so exhausting and wrought with tensions that home education began to fall by the wayside and the public schools to sound like salvation. The perpetual westward migration of citizens meant the breakdown of the extended-family households that had been the backbone of family learning. Common people, fearing the influx of immigrants to their country, looked to the schools to integrate newcomers in a way industrialized communities couldn't. Finally, the growth of industry so altered the economic landscape that parents no longer trusted themselves as the bedrock of a child's learning. Schools began to seem to them necessary if their children were going to "get ahead." The result was loss of family control over both the content and manner of education, but as time passed more and more Americans found themselves willing to accept such a condition.

The common-school crusade in its early stages had been mostly about elementary schooling, but it quickly encompassed and gave impetus to the drive toward state-controlled secondary schools. Again Massachusetts led the way: Nearly one hundred high schools were established in the Commonwealth by the middle of the nineteenth century. And again the crusaders met stiff resistance from common people: In Beverly, Massachusetts, the vast majority of the town's working people voted in 1860 to abolish the town's new high school. The critical moment, though, came in 1872, when a Michigan taxpayer sued his local school district to prevent it from collecting taxes in support of high schools. The state's supreme court unanimously upheld the district's right to levy such taxes and thus established a precedent for other states. By the turn of the century the public schools, both elementary and secondary, were firmly entrenched in the life of the nation and had pervasively usurped the family's role in providing for the education of children.

About this, as I have said, there are at least two common interpretations. The one most historians favor is that the young nation, in the spirit of democracy, had established schools that were free to all regardless of creed or financial status. Others assert that the nation's egalitarian ideology was subverted by the industrialists who stood behind the common-school crusaders, supporting them with financial and political firepower: They wanted to *compel* children to be trained to the needs of industry and to the requirements of the modern nation state. Somewhere between, perhaps, lies the truth. The new schools were free of charge, but they were also compulsory. The opportunity they provided was mandatory.

With free public schools firmly established, the question of what sort of schools they ought to be—how they should be structured, what should be taught in them—soon took center stage. The debate, of course, had always been present: as far back as 1844 Mann had clashed with Boston schoolmasters who preferred corporal punishment and stern Puritan authority to kindness, understanding, and mutual respect between teachers and students. Chiefly, though, questions about what the new schools should be were answered not by idealists such as Mann but by bureaucratic imperatives. Efficient management swiftly became an end in its own right, one that had a way of overwhelming notions about how best to educate.

The bureaucrats of the new schools were not long in making their presence felt: "age-graded" classrooms took the place of classrooms where children of varying ages had mixed; standardized textbooks, selected by state education boards, were disseminated throughout school systems; teaching was professionalized, and states took it upon themselves to certify all who would presume to educate; cost efficiency became the catchword in the operation of schools. The vision of the public schools fell to administrators and state officials, and control over them shifted from parents and communities to bureaucrats and "professionals."

By the turn of the century a group of liberal progressives—John Dewey, Jane Addams, and Francis Parker, among others—were busily criticizing the common schools. They aimed at rehumanizing an increasingly inhumane modern society, particularly its educational institutions. The status quo was rote memorization and recitation in classrooms thronged with passive children who were sternly disciplined when they expressed individual needs. The black-and-white photographs of this era in education are ingrained in our collective national psyche: rows of students seated stiffly at high wooden desks while frowning Miss Grundy, pointer in hand, listens grimly to a youth in a starched collar reciting multiplication tables. No one looks very happy about anything. No one seems to want to be there.

Dewey led the way in articulating reforms that would address the nightmare schools had become. In Dewey's eyes the public schools, established in the name of democracy, no longer took into account the dignity and value of every human being. They had become, instead, isolated institutions increasingly divorced from community life and increasingly regimented in their treatment of children. The classroom, Dewey thought, should be a "miniature society" reflective of the larger one; when it was autocratic, stern, inflexible, and a burden to the spirit, utterly insensible to individual needs, it could not and did not reflect democracy. Schools had fostered the delusion that education was a means to an end, a process that terminated upon graduation and that had as its raison d'être the preparation of children for life in the working world. On the contrary, Dewey argued, education was a continuous and ceaseless process that was part and parcel of one's existence from birth to grave.

Dewey gave fresh voice to Rousseau's child-centered notion: Schools should meet the needs of each child, not the other way around. Dewey's Laboratory School, established at the University of Chicago in 1896, dismantled the rigid curricula of the nineteenth century and replaced them with activities that inspired and cultivated the interests of individual children. Its successes, though, inspired only grudging reform of a limited sort in the realm of the common school; while many educational theorists jumped on Dewey's bandwagon, most administrators did not. By the twenties, state schools had become so unwieldy that nobody could figure out how to make them change; lip service to change was thus far easier than change itself. Dewey was celebrated as the father of modern American education, but his ideas for flexible and child-centered schools were not widely enacted, and the loud talk of reform was mostly rhetorical. Classrooms remained crowded, curricula remained standardized, efficiency kept the upper hand in its battle with new ideas. Little, in short, really changed.

Meanwhile, with immigration and an exploding national population the public-school system became bloated and its funding evolved into the political issue it is today. If a politician wished to be reelected he had to promise to keep taxes at bay, and this naturally exerted a downward pull on school funding. By Pearl Harbor the Depression had gutted progressivism and reduced it to little beyond the occasional field trip proffered to schoolchildren in the spirit of Dewey—in order to have a progressive experience, it seems, one had to *leave* school for the day. The advent of the Cold War did nothing to change this nor did the spirit of conformity and materialism, the unabashed normalcy, of the 1950s. It was not until the new era of the sixties rolled around that educators began once again to worship at the altar of Rousseau and Dewey. But they, like their predecessors, were naive in believing that child-centered education was viable in public-school classrooms.

The sixties was a vigorous era in education, a period in which alternatives to conventional schools flourished for a season and then died or fell by the wayside. Free schools, block schools, group schools, open schools—the terminology differed wherever you went, but the philosophical premises rarely did: Rousseau and Dewey were right, claimed the new educators, and their ideas should be enacted in our nation's schools even if so doing meant radical change.

So radical changes were made at such places as the Morgan Community School in Washington, D.C., the Underwood School in Newton, Massachusetts, and the East Harlem Block

School in New York City, all purveyors of the *open-school* concept. A book entitled *Doing Your Own School*—written in 1972 by the Great Atlantic and Pacific School Conspiracy, which announced beneath its roll call of names that the book's royalties would "go in part for support of The Learning Place, a free junior and senior high school in San Francisco, and The Group School, a working-class high school in Cambridge, Mass."—describes open schools this way:

It's hard to say just when school actually begins because there is very little organized activity for the whole class. You may see a small group of children working on mathematics or reading, but most children are on their own. . . . There is no special time for separate subjects in the curriculum, and no real difference between work and play. In fact, these schools are based in part on the notion that what adults call play is the principal means of learning in childhood. . . .

Generally, teachers start the day by listing available activities. A child might spend the day on his first choice or he might not. Although there is a commitment to letting the children choose freely, in practice many teachers give work when they think it's needed. But to a very great extent the children really have a choice and go purposefully about their work.

The classrooms are fairly noisy because the children can move and talk freely, and sometimes the teacher has to ask for quiet. However, when children work independently, discipline becomes less a problem than it is in more formal classrooms. When the class is taught as a unit, and every child is supposed to pay attention as the teacher talks, discipline can be a very serious matter.

Quick children get restless; slow children are bored. In an open classroom, most children are usually absorbed, and those who are restless may go outdoors or play in the hallways.

The extent to which these alternative classrooms contain the seeds of their own destruction is readily apparent in *Doing Your Own School*: Its authors, while celebrating it, are already apologizing that the open classroom in practice is not the open classroom in theory and that discipline and assigned work have had to rear their ugly heads. Later they confess that during the first year of the East Harlem Block School "the curriculum and structure were that of a free school. The parents later rejected this model because the children were not making sufficient progress in learning the basic skills of reading and arithmetic." Not until the midseventies, however, was the widespread failure of the alternative-education movement acknowledged by all but a few diehards. They pressed on, mostly as directors of private schools, occasionally as administrators of public alternative schools that involved—and still involve—only a small percentage of the school-going population. But for the most part the alternative movement had had its day, short-lived, with little real impact on the vast mainstream of education; the public-school classroom remained almost everywhere predictable, routine, and dull.

If anything, the failures of the alternative movement gave conservative educators the grist they needed to generate a post-sixties, back-to-basics educational agenda. These failures also prevented many educators from listening seriously to critics of the schools—such people as Paul Goodman, Jonathan Kozol, Herbert Kohl, James Herndon, George Dennison, Ivan Illich, and John Holt, among others—who articulated in the sixties and seventies a position similar to the one Dewey and the progressives had staked out earlier: that conventional schools stifled the individual and that mass institutions of learning, with their attendant managerial and bureaucratic headaches, could not properly educate our young.

But while educators largely ignored these critics, a small number of parents began to listen, among them early homeschoolers. In fact, the contemporary progressive homeschooling movement—a grass-roots phenomenon—can be traced back to this period of the midseventies, a time in which many were finally concluding what Holt in particular had come to conclude: that alternative schools did not often work and that public schools could not be meaningfully reformed as long as they remained mass institutions. In 1977 Holt founded *Growing Without Schooling*, a forum in print for the exchange of ideas about home education. By the fourth issue he had five hundred subscribers; by the tenth he had received ten thousand letters. In 1987 Patricia Lines, a policy analyst with the Department of Education, estimated that as many as 260,000 children were being homeschooled in the United States. By 1990, according to one report, that number had doubled, and the national press could no longer ignore them, especially when homeschooling children began to succeed—reaching the final round of a state spelling bee, for example, or enrolling at such colleges as Harvard.

From a historical perspective it is possible to assert that these half a million children are no mere oddity. Homeschoolers are not eccentrics and cranks but keepers of an educational tradition that sustained human beings for thousands of years and Americans until the mid-nineteenth century. State-controlled, compulsory schools, on the other hand, are a relatively recent phenomenon, a modern educational experiment whose results, thus far, are not particularly encouraging. Their failures result in large degree from their neglect of two long-standing historical truths: that parents are natural educators and that family life is crucial to educational success. Perhaps in the next century we will at last find ways to embed these truths in our public system of education, which is currently in desperate need of them.

6

Abiding Questions

If you are going to keep your children out of schools you had better decide what an education *means* because no one is going to do it for you. Plato maintained that an education allowed a man to grasp forms, Aquinas that it allowed him to contemplate God, Locke that it filled his tabula rasa with virtue, wisdom, breeding, and learning. Rousseau's educated man was spontaneous and free, Marx's accountable and communal in spirit, Buber's an existentialist. For Dewey and his fellow pragmatists, education was largely a social matter, the educated man one who became reflective about his society. Meanwhile, in our own time, B. F. Skinner and the behaviorists have conceived of the educated man as a well-trained product, a result of strict scientific engineering designed to yield a conditioned citizen. In short, theorists and philosophers have never agreed on the purpose of an education. Their disagreement, it turns out, is reflected in our public schools, which have haphazardly incorporated a little of everything and which lack a coherent philosophy.

Admittedly, coming to conclusions about educational philosophy is difficult for anybody. Every camp—analytic, existential, pragmatic, and so forth—has had more than a little to say about it. Our schools have ended up with a mixed bag, but they have also been subject to those currents of thought that have been most forceful, generally, in other aspects of Western life. In other words, Plato and Aristotle have counted more in our schools than Sartre, Saint Augustine, or the Bhagavad Gita. Homeschoolers, meanwhile, have found an affinity for Rousseau and for twentieth-century thinkers of a child-centered bent: Dewey, Ivan Illich, and John Holt. Other educational philosophers have mattered deeply to both schools and homeschools, but Plato, Aristotle, Rousseau, Dewey, Illich, and Holt have been central. Robin and I, finding ourselves with no school to rely on, plunged into them relucantly: educational philosophy is big and forces a person to begin somewhere. We were looking to formulate our own educational principles and to address those basic educational questions philosophers have so much written about. What is the highest purpose of an education? What is the nature or definition of knowledge? How might we define the educated individual? What might we all agree is true, and what might the answer have to do with us, our sons, our lives?

Few writers, we soon found, are as unreadable as philosophers, who traffic in abstractions about abstractions and who intentionally, it seems, weary their readers with endless asides, perambulations, commentaries, and digressions. One result is that philosophy has gone out of fashion and we have as a nation turned to pop psychology—Leo Buscaglia on living and loving—to do what philosophy once did. Where today is there a genuine philosopher to whom the average American is inclined to listen? Philosophers have written themselves straight out of the mainstream of life and are now viewed as pointy-headed anachronisms: Do we even *have* philosophers anymore? At the end of the twentieth century we have abandoned philosophy— or it has abandoned us—and this is as true in the world of education as it is everywhere else. In fact, I know of very few teachers who have, for example, read Plato, not to mention Dewey or Rousseau. Those who have are generally chagrined that the schools they work in have few guiding philosophic principles and many bureaucratic ones. Administrators are even less inclined than teachers to have a cursory understanding of the philosophical foundations of learning. Principals and superintendents pass their working lives absorbed in those matters institutions require—public relations, money management, organizational tactics—instead of implementing an educational vision. The result is that no one has seen to it that our public schools have a vision, despite the endless committee and board meetings convened, presumably, with such a purpose in mind.

For a century and a half now we have had a public-school system based on unexamined and inconsistent premises. To begin with—and like so much else in the Western world—schools are a product of platonic idealism, a term denoting the preeminence of ideas: ideas, Plato wrote, are eternal, reliable, while the physical world is temporary and uncertain. An education, he added, ought to be about the search for truths so irrefutable, so absolute, that they could weather forever the mutability of this planet: Two plus two equals four is a truth, as are geometric proofs, the laws that govern algebra and calculus, the principles of Newtonian mechanics and the rules of formal logic ("All men are mortal, Socrates is a man, thus Socrates is mortal"). Plato's curriculum called for students to liberate themselves from the imperfect world and to commit instead to an abstract world on a plane above ordinary life. What mattered most was the theoretical, rules, laws, and principles that lifted one out of this world and into the world of absolutes.

Platonic idealism gradually permeated almost every aspect of Western life, chief among them our institutions of learning.

Our schools do part of what Plato hoped they would: They promote abstraction over physical reality. Textbook questions on the surface of the moon are substituted for the moon as seen through a telescope; work sheets on trees, their leaves, branches, bark, and roots are substituted for living birches. In this manner schools alienate children from earth, life, even from themselves, and shape them into adults short on reverence for the world and perpetually buffered from it.

Our schools inherited from platonic philosophy not only their abstract curriculum but their hierarchical structure—in short, their primary traits. Plato envisioned a class society based on one's ability to grasp the truths that lay beyond this world; rulers—philosopher-kings—would be drawn from those most adept at it. Schools would cull those with a talent for abstraction from the herd of plodding materialists unfit for anything but manual labor. The ability to abstract would replace bloodlines as the deciding factor in one's future.

Plato also called for vigorous state interest in education. Since the state will draw its leaders from schools it should take an active role in them, he wrote in *The Republic*. School and government should be inextricably bound, politics and education linked in order to ensure the maintenance of a stable class society. In these matters we have obliged Plato as well.

Abstraction, hierarchy, education under the auspices of the state: The platonic scheme, surely, has had much influence on our own. What is glaringly missing from our version, however, is the platonic method, the dialectic, in which the vigorous clash of differing points of view inspires revelation. Instead, students only rarely offer opinions or trade ideas in our school classrooms, and most instructional time is devoted to teacher-directed activities and to the earnest droning of the teacher's voice.

Our schools inherit from Plato, then, the worst of what he has to offer: the tracking, testing, measuring, and grading that are central to a hierarchical institution; and the work sheets, lectures, study guides, and texts essential to their abstract nature. Schools offer far too much theoretical math, blackboard science, workbook geography, and textbook history. The best of Plato—meaningful discussion, the dialectic, the give and take of important ideas—turns out to be impractical in large institutions (and perhaps more than impractical: Bertrand Russell once observed that the United States was the world's only major nation to deliberately avoid teaching its children to think dialectically). Thirty children brought together for a one-hour English class only rarely engage in the sort of dialectic that might truly advance their educations. Most of them—teachers know this—will simply defer to the loquacious minority, their chins in their hands, one eye on the clock, and wait the period out.

While many of Plato's ideas on education have been incorporated into the structure of modern schools, Plato would no doubt feel dismay sitting in a modern classroom. He would find that despite the high level of abstraction—the "imperfect" real world safely outside school walls—students are asked to memorize facts disconnected from the larger ideas that give them meaning. They are taught specific skills such as word processing and keyboarding while their grasp of vital concepts, their broader understanding, receives secondary attention. In history and English classes they memorize specifics—Civil War battles, Romantic poets—but often gain no deeper insight into history or poetry, make no connection between dates, names, places, themes, and the larger currents they suggest. Plato would be dismayed to find that modern schools are abstract places prodding students toward the limited and material. Is it any wonder they don't work well? No consistent philosophy, idealist, or any other guides them toward successful principles of operation. Plato, in the end, would be confused by them.

Idealists like Plato (Descartes, Berkeley, Kant, and Hegel have all in turn taken up the platonic cause, and Alfred North Whitehead once remarked that Western philosophy is but a series of footnotes to the ancient Greek avatar of absolute truth) have been countered by a school of realists and materialists harkening all the way back to Aristotle, Plato's most prominent pupil. Realists accept the profound significance of ideas without dismissing, at the same time, substance; a systematic study of *this* world, they say, yields insight into the world of abstract truth that can be gleaned in no other way. Aristotle in particular felt that the unique properties of an object—an acorn, a conch shell, the antlers of an elk—were clues to the universal, and the realists in general have promoted methodical science, close examination of physical reality, and the systematic categorizing and cataloging of knowledge. Bacon and Locke, both of whom championed the inductive method (deriving general truths from a study of particulars), and in our own century Whitehead and Russell have all taken their cues from Aristotle.

In the realm of education the realists have had much to say, and their preoccupation with categorizing and classifying knowledge is apparent in the curriculum of our schools. The notion of biology as distinct from chemistry or of literature as distinct from history is Aristotelian in essence, and while these distinctions help students to mark clear boundaries they also prevent them from making clear connections. From realists—whose educational philosophy is most concerned with the transmission of vast amounts of well-ordered facts—we get the hour-per-subject design of the modern high school, the teacher at his podium methodically spewing information, the objective test (did the information "imprint"?), and the emphasis on rote memorization and passive learning still central to the public-school curriculum. In desperate times our schools turn with desperation to realism, which now goes by the name of back-to-basics education and which emphasizes standardized tests and objective measures of accountability. The real must be quantifiable.

For progressive homeschoolers the realists are disconcerting, the idealists interesting, and romantic naturalists such as Jean-Jacques Rousseau worth singular attention. Many seem to have discovered Rousseau only after the fact and found in him a ready philosophical voice for what they were already doing. Rousseau, as I have pointed out, felt parents should protect children from the ill effects of civilization and carefully nurture their innate goodness. He advocated removing them from institutions, keeping them from books until twelve years of age, and cultivating their emotions as more vital than their intellects. For Rousseau experience, not the classroom, was preeminent: The world itself—its woodlands, farms, clerks, and laborers—would best educate a child. Homeschoolers, of course, feel an affinity for this point of view, which leads children away from schools and textbooks and into everyday life. For those of an isolationist bent, prone to suspicion of society in general and given to protecting their children from it, Rousseau's belief in the basic goodness of children and in the corrupting energy of civilization affirms their parental impulses. Rousseau was primarily concerned with what was "natural"; homeschoolers have extrapolated much from this, including that young children are not naturally inclined to sit in desks for long periods each day, focus their minds on perpetual abstractions, remain quiet, control their limbs. Children are much more naturally inclined, when given a choice, to run, jump, skip, and play, and to absorb themselves in whatever engages their instinctive curiosity. These observations accord with those of most parents and educators, of course. Our schools nevertheless remain at odds with them, partly because of institutional imperatives, partly in the name of "preparing children for the adult world."

Still, the sentimental romanticism and ill-considered permissiveness we see in some homeschooling families is not Rousseauian at all. To those who actually read his work it is clear that Rousseau did not intend for children to run, jump, skip, and play all day in a never-never land of eternal fun where every whim is attended to. Rousseau takes pains to point out, instead, that an education should be guided by a child's natural interest in the world—not merely her whims—and that adults must take upon themselves the responsibility of nurturing that interest. Not to do so, to claim one's child pursues her whims all day long because Rousseau suggests it ought to be so, is not only a gross misreading of his work but also a strategy for educational failure and an abdication of parental responsibility.

Dewey, like Rousseau, is both much spoken of and much misunderstood among progressive homeschoolers. Like Rousseau, Dewey considered the child's interests central to his or her education, and like Rousseau he has been taken by homeschoolers to mean that adults should defer to children's whims. (Dewey, incidentally, once wrote of Rousseau that while authoring *Emile* he "was allowing his own children to grow up entirely neglected by their parents, abandoned in a foundling asylum. It is strange, then, that his readers and students should center their interest in his theories, in his general contribution to education, rather than in his account of the impractical methods he used to create that exemplary prig—Emile." To put it another way, Dewey did not always follow Rousseau's lead.) Teachers have misunderstood Dewey, too, but generally their confusion hasn't mattered too much—his child-centered, progressive approach is at odds with the bureaucratic nature of the institution they work in. It is ironic, then, that there are those in either camp, homeschoolers and public educators both, who see Dewey as their patron philosopher. These muddled loyalties are perhaps partly Dewey's fault: he is not only the most significant American educational philosopher but also the most unreadable.

The essence of Dewey is progressive, finally, though Dewey was often critical of progressivism as it was practiced in the public schools. Dewey believed that modern life had damaged not only the individual but society, and that it was therefore the job of modern schools both to nurture individuals and to repair the unraveling social fabric. Schools, he said, should liberate the individual to take part meaningfully in social and democratic processes. He did not see this going forward in American public education, and for the most part he denounced the ostensibly child-centered and progressive reforms sometimes carried out in his name. Still, homeschoolers misinterpret Dewey if they imagine his philosophy sanctions the withdrawal of their children from schools. Dewey was finally a great believer in institutions; he felt certain that schools could inspire individuals to take satisfaction in constructive social lives. As a progressive he held out enormous hope that schools could one day significantly reform a troubled society.

Nevertheless, many homeschoolers claim to take their cues from Dewey as well as from others of a child-centered bent, among them Johann Pestalozzi, Friedrich Froebel, Maria Montessori, Rudolf Steiner, and A. S. Neill. While these educators have championed the primacy of the child, none has suggested that schools should be abandoned or that families should abandon schools. That extreme view was given voice in our own time by the founding father of the homeschooling movement,

John Holt, and by his more scholarly and radical contemporary Ivan Illich: the twin towers of—if there is such a thing—progressive homeschooling philosophy.

One can best discern what Illich is about in his 1970 book *Deschooling Society*, a sophisticated tirade against all things modern weighed down by revolutionary political rhetoric and by an abstract approach to educational problems. For children of the sixties who themselves had children, Illich provided the philosophical basis for continuing the revolution into parenthood. In schools, he informs us, "all students are academically processed to be happy only in the company of fellow consumers of the products of the educational machine. . . . School," he adds elsewhere, "has become the world religion of a modernized proletariat, and makes futile promises of salvation to the poor of the technological age." Illich struck a chord with disillusioned neo-Luddites who found in institutions such as schools the virus that had infected civilized humanity and that had to be destroyed before humanity could recover.

Deschooling Society advanced the point of view that institutions themselves are the problem—it doesn't seem to matter how they are shaped—and that the single best solution to our educational problems is to dismantle institutions of learning. The power of schools to regulate our lives, to define our learning, shape our purposes, dictate our standards, and determine our careers should be destroyed once and for all, says Illich; the result would be liberation of the individual from institutional tyranny, a more vigorous society, a deeper and richer cultural imagination, and an open community of learning. The message has some attractions worth pondering; the pedantic rhetoric does not. Illich was not listened to by many Americans and has not had the impact of, say, Marshall McLuhan or Buckminster Fuller (two notable deep thinkers from the same era), in part because he was incomprehensible, in part because his ideas for educational reform presupposed the sort of radical social change few Americans were inclined to make. Finally, too, Illich was more concerned with the society that would emerge when schools were abandoned than with education in its own right. He called for a cultural revolution in America that could only begin once schools were gone, but he remained both vague and unrealistic about the educational arrangements that would take their place.

Illich's contemporary, the educator John Holt, had already published four significant books by the time *Deschooling Society* appeared. In his fifth, *Freedom and Beyond*, Holt allied himself with Illich in calling for a deschooled society, but he said:

> by a deschooled society we don't mean a society without any arrangements and resources for learning. . . . We don't even mean a society without any schools. Some things—languages, music, dance—may be better learned in a school than in any other way, or may even require a school. . . . But in a deschooled society, nobody would be compelled to go to school. . . . No one would be punished for not liking schools, not finding them good places to learn, and not learning there, or for wanting and trying to learn in other ways. . . . In sum, a deschooled society would be a society in which everyone shall have the widest and freest possible choice to learn whatever he wants to learn, whether in school or in some altogether different way.

Holt, of course, was talking about homeschooling emerging as a pervasive phenomenon. His central notion, like Dewey's and Rousseau's, was that the child's interests should dictate his education; unlike Dewey he came to the conclusion that this was improbable in schools. In fact, from one point of view it is possible to say that Holt and Dewey are diametrically opposed, the former calling for educational self-sufficiency, the latter for schools as democratic institutions inspiring social cooperation. Dewey believed that "what the best and wisest parent wants for his own child, that must the community want for all its children"; Holt, certainly, would not disagree but gave his energies to parents and communities instead of to institutions. For so doing he has been criticized as "retreat[ing] from any collective consideration of educational ideals" and as "dismiss[ing] the idea that communities have any educational responsibilities to their members." His supporters have replied that withdrawal from classrooms is not the same as withdrawal from communal responsibility for education and that advocating family as a venue for learning is not the same as promoting social disintegration. Nevertheless Holt, like Rousseau and Dewey before him, has often been misunderstood. He has been called naive for swallowing whole certain notions central to Rousseau's naturalistic philosophy (that nature is good, that civilization is bad, that social life corrupts, that children are noble savages). He has been labeled everything from radical to reactionary and has been attacked as an elitist promoting the neglect of America's underclass in favor of the imperative to "teach your own" (even though Holt was a lifelong advocate for the poor and disenfranchised). Finally, those who take his call for parental commitment to children's learning as an assault on American education have, perhaps, willfully misread him. When Holt gave up on school reform and committed his energies to the homeschooling movement, he was looking for ways to give more Americans access to a better education.

But Holt has not done a better job of putting educational questions to rest than other theorists and philosophers. What is the purpose of education? How do we recognize the educated individual? Should education serve the individual or society? What things are worth teaching, what things are worth learning, what role should formal instruction play, what place should ordinary experience have in the education of our young? What is the nature of the human mind, of truth, knowledge, matter, perception?

An obsession with philosophical questions such as these might lead us hourly away from our children, away from the work of educating them and from important, daily decisions about how best to take part in their learning. This doesn't mean, though, that we should turn away from philosophy altogether as a distraction from the real work at hand. We need to reflect on those philosophical issues that seem pertinent to the work of educating children and, more important, act on our conclusions about them. If not we leave it to somebody else to answer these abiding questions for us.

7

The Matter of Money

No argument for homeschooling is cogent to Ned Hall, a friend who insists with polite amusement that all discussion of the subject is superfluous. For Ned, a carpenter, as for others we know, the significant facts about homeschooling are economic, and the fact that seems to him most significant of all is that Americans work for a living. Americans have jobs, Ned points out, that take them from their homes and families.

Homeschooling, Ned adds, may or may not be a good thing, but in the end our thoughts about it are wholly irrelevant, our feelings utterly beside the point, because tomorrow, early, we must get up and go to work, leaving our children to the schools. Tomorrow, as today, we will not have a choice, chiefly because we must work.

End, for Ned, of conversation.

Ned is right that money has a way of superseding everything else. But suppose, for a moment, that one's thoughts about education mattered, that one's feelings were not beside the point, and that our economy were arranged to make involvement in a child's education the prerogative of every parent. Suppose that for those who desired such involvement the economic mechanisms were in place to make it feasible. Would our economy—would we—indeed suffer?

Ned might respond that the question is irrelevant: too roomy, too abstract, too hypothetical. Ned might point out that he and his wife, a Seattle ophthalmologist's receptionist and secretary, have a mortgage and two cars, a checkbook they must balance, a daughter in college and a retirement fund: They can't start homeschooling tomorrow. There is no possibility of rearranging their lives in order to homeschool next year, either —assuming the two of them wanted to. ("We don't," Ned emphasizes.) "Back in the fifties," he explains, "back then maybe people could have homeschooled. Maybe back then, when somebody stayed home all day. Back when people could afford houses on one salary, a long time ago, when we were kids."

Ned rightly points to a new fact about our economic life: In more than 85 percent of American households either both parents now work or a single parent does, a condition that has altered our social landscape fundamentally and in deeply troubling ways. Americans have gradually come to recognize this and have begun to reconsider their working lives; many are now pondering whether their jobs or careers haven't undermined or hampered their families. Some have sought to reconcile work and family but thus far with only limited success: maternal, paternal, and pregnancy leaves, bereavement leaves and job-sharing arrangements, greater flexibility for part-time employees, and, in Oregon, recently enacted legislation that provides workers with twelve weeks of biannual leave to care for seriously ill family members. Yet despite these inroads many remain disturbed by how work continues to usurp those energies they would prefer to reserve for family life. Oregon's commissioner for labor and industries, Mary Wendy Roberts, describes the United States as "the last hold-out of the world's industrial countries against making a formal, national commitment to families." Leave to care for ill family members, she points out, is available in such economic powers as Japan and Germany. "Their experience," she adds, "proves that accommodating the family needs of their work forces does not lead to national economic ruin."

Our business leaders will reply that they can nevertheless ill afford the kind of openness that would allow workers to home-school. They once said the same about the minimum wage, about child-labor laws and the eight-hour day, about pregnancy, paternity, and maternity leaves—the needs of families, their argument goes, cost them money in the form of lost work hours, which ultimately costs the rest of us in the form of higher prices, fewer jobs, recession. The rest of us might argue in response that we pay far greater costs, both socially and economically, when families are rent apart by financial realities that force the vast majority of parents into the workplace. Our society must bear the costs that inevitably accrue when children are cut adrift from family life and left to fend, psychologically and emotionally, for themselves.

Such a line of thought has not been particularly popular in America since the advent, in the late sixties, of the women's movement. Great progress has been made since then toward establishing the principle of equal access for both genders in the workplace, and women now report taking enormous satisfaction from careers and professions once closed to them. This has been the work of many years, not to be taken lightly nor obstructed thoughtlessly. At the same time, Americans should recognize that the movement of millions of women into the work force has meant a diminution of family life and an enormous increase in the kinds of social problems—crime, drug use, illiteracy—that inevitably result when men have not chosen, in any numbers worth speaking about, to step in and do what women once did. In short, no one is home anymore.

None of this, however, means that women who work should be encouraged to return to their homes and children simply because they are women. Rather, parents of both sexes might reconsider how their working lives influence the lives of their children.

Feminists have been right in pointing out that "pro-family" rhetoric is often little more than veiled women bashing. Right-wing politicians, eager to jump on the family bandwagon, frequently use family as a bat with which to beat working women, and family at election time becomes a political catchword rather than a web of meaningful relationships that matter deeply to those engaged in them. Family, for advertisers, is a nostalgic and often romantic idea rather than a daily reality. Like baseball, hot dogs, and Chevrolet pickup trucks, family is a powerful *image*. It sells, among other things, antifreeze, Volvos, car batteries, Thanksgiving turkeys, detergents, and dishwashing machines.

It is easy, then, for thoughtful people to be suspicious of those who, like myself, call for a reconsideration of our working lives in light of our lives as parents. Such a reconsideration is a political act, tied as much to the history of the women's movement as to the imagery of election campaigns. It is also a far deeper matter that rightly includes our reflections on human instincts, on the influence of culture and economics on family life, and on our personal mores and principles. Politicians and advertisers may have appropriated family, but that doesn't mean everyone else should thumb their noses at it. In the end, work versus family might best be thought of as an unfortunate modern antagonism—historical, cultural, and economic in origin, its roots far deeper than the strata of contemporary social issues in which it is generally discussed.

Hey, all well and good, says Ned Hall. But listen, I have to go to work now. Maybe we can talk about this during the weekend sometime. . . .

Business leaders have a valid point about staying home to teach one's own: It differs fundamentally from maternity leave, family illness leave, all leaves. Homeschooling is not any sort of "leave" at all but a permanent state of affairs. Employees who want to homeschool are not asking for three months or six months away from work; they are asking, instead, to arrange their working lives in such a manner that there is time, each day, for perhaps eighteen years, to take an active role in educating their children. This is an ongoing arrangement business has thus far been reluctant to provide, and it is furthermore an arrangement most Americans cannot afford, for we have somehow arrived at a juncture in our economic history where there is no longer time for children and where in many cases both parents must work away from home—without any help from an extended family—merely to keep a roof over their heads. Employees who would prefer to arrange their lives so that more time is available for educating their children are thus prevented not only by inflexible employers but by the financial realities of the times in which we live. Americans, in short, can't afford to homeschool, however desirable it might be as a method for teaching their young.

This state of affairs seems particularly ironic in an age widely characterized as postindustrial and in a country where, increasingly, homes and offices are linked to each other by modems, fax machines, and computer networks. In fact, at no time in the past one hundred years has working at home been as feasible as it is today, when many Americans hold the kinds of jobs that do not really require a daily commute to a central place of business. Many are in a position to work flexible hours at home where they can do their work electronically, save the hours spent bogged down in traffic, and give more attention to their families. Whereas the industrial age meant adults left home to work in the plants and factories, the information age might well mean that many are free, should they so desire, to work at home again.

Just as new technologies challenge us to ponder whether commuting to centralized places of business is anymore a financial requirement, they should also cause us to rethink schools. In the nineteenth century family life did not often include the kinds of raw materials—books, maps, globes, scientific apparatus—one found characteristically in classrooms. Schools provided information about the world beyond the family and transported young people to places and times to which they would otherwise have had no access. Today, however, much has changed, and the vast majority of American homes have, at the least, televisions and radios to bring the world to them. Many homes are also plentifully supplied with books, magazines, newspapers, and educational software; before too long the contents of entire libraries will be available via computer terminals to every home in America. Home is no longer necessarily the kind of information vacuum that once made school seem mandatory; it can now be not only a fully stocked repository of information but also a far cheaper venue for education than the vast institutions we currently construct at great expense to taxpayers. Consider the cost-effectiveness of using existing sites—homes—versus the expense of maintaining or building schools. Consider, also, the enormous savings to taxpayers of using a highly skilled labor force—parents—to do what "professional" teachers now do. The more parents who teach, the fewer teachers, administrators, classrooms, and offices that must be paid for at public expense. Tax dollars available for educational purposes could then be put to far better uses than building new buildings and hiring more "professionals." They could be used, for example, to encourage a commitment to education in every family and to provide families short on educational resources with the raw materials and assistance they need.

In fact, teaching one's own might be far more affordable if our government-run schools were not so wasteful and did not deplete such an enormous share of our public tax monies. In Washington State nearly half of every tax dollar is spent on kindergarten through twelfth-grade education; in New York City a seven-billion-dollar school budget produces students who can't read or solve basic math problems or write much beyond their own names. New York State's Teacher of the Year for 1991, John Taylor Gatto, sheds light on how this came to be:

> Out of every dollar allocated to New York schools 51% is removed at the top for system-wide administrative costs. Local school districts remove another 5% for district administrative costs. At the school site there is wide latitude [concerning] what to do with the remaining 44%, but the average school deducts another 12% more for administration and supervision, bringing the total deducted from our dollar to 68 cents. But there are more non-teaching costs in most schools: coordinators of all sorts, guidance counselors, librarians, honorary administrators who are relieved of teaching duties to do favors for listed administrators . . . under these flexible guidelines the 32 cents remaining after three administrative levies is dropped in most schools to a quarter, two bits. Out of a 7 billion dollar school budget this is a net loss to instruction from all other uses equalling 5½ billion dollars.

Some homeschoolers argue that the $7,300 per student New York collects from taxpayers for "educational purposes" might better be returned to families—in the form of a tax break, credit, or voucher—in order to help alleviate their financial burdens and allow them to educate their own. Losers, they say, would be educational administrators, who often make more than twice as much as teachers; winners would be everybody else. Americans would benefit from the improved quality of education at no greater tax cost than is currently borne, and in the long run taxpayers would actually save money as more parents began to teach their own and the need for new school construction diminished. Meanwhile, in families with two school-age children the returned, say, $10,000 (the remaining $4,600 could be reserved to the state for the cost of program evaluation, resources, and expertise, and as supplementary funding for public schools) would allow a fundamental change in the working lives of parents: One or both might work part time, and the hours away from work could be devoted to educating their children more effectively than New York City does.

Such straight-thinking pragmatists as my friend Ned Hall are especially offended by such ideas. Tax credits for homeschoolers seem to Ned unconstitutional, since they would provide state funding to home "private schools" sometimes religious in nature. They would also, to Ned's thinking, drive a nail into the coffin of our public-education system, which would suffer dearly from the loss of funds and from the absence of students from families committed to education. Finally, the potential for abuse of such a tax credit is enormous: If Ned is right, we can expect that in many instances returned funds would be used for purposes other than education. Ned admits he would find himself tempted to pocket his tax-credit money and go right on working full time as a carpenter while his children fended educationally for themselves.

Despite the objections of people such as Ned (and of homeschoolers who fear tax credits will increase governmental control over what they do), tax-credit, tax-voucher, and school-choice plans are gaining currency in educational circles and are now even promoted by the federal government, which can no longer ignore the simple fact that private schools—at far lower cost—do a better job of educating than public ones. The same, of course, is true of homeschools, which currently cost taxpayers nothing.

Ned might worry that school-choice plans produce inequality and segregation; if so he should look closely at circumstances in Kansas City, where black families are fighting in federal court to force the public schools to provide scholarships to private ones. The city's public schools, like most urban public schools, are academically inferior to its private ones; those who can afford to—three out of four whites and a sprinkling of minority students—have fled their halls altogether. Meanwhile, Kansas City's private schools stand ready to accept more than four thousand new minority students into their integrated student bodies. These private schools spend about $2,000 per pupil; Kansas City spends about $6,000. Yet clearly the private schools have created a more desirable learning environment, one better integrated and academically effective. With scholarships or tax credits the disadvantaged in our society would gain access to such private schools, which are currently available only to those who can afford them. If anything, proponents of such strategies argue, tax credits would produce greater equality and less segregation than restricting the disadvantaged to public schools only. And credits for homeschoolers would merely increase the range of choice, providing families of all sorts with even more options.

Yet tax credits, however attractive to some, put learning on the marketplace, where learning does not belong. Business leaders would have us view education as a service industry, schools as competing service providers, students and families as paying consumers—the idea being that education will improve once market mechanisms govern it. In fact, the entrenched belief in market forces as a remedy for shoddy products and services ("Look at the Soviets," business leaders used to advise, before pointing out that our public schools constitute a government monopoly on education) is not easily translated to the realm of learning, a realm business leaders almost never understand. Instead they speak of learning in the language of business—competition, investment, accountability, performance—as if their metaphors indeed applied to children.

Yet business leaders, for their own reasons, are ultimately as concerned as anyone else about the quality of American education. The California Business Roundtable and the Minnesota Business Partnership have spearheaded the reform of schools in their respective states, and the Committee for Economic Development—a powerful group of corporate leaders—has issued a major policy statement entitled *Investing in Our Children: Business and the Public Schools*. Meanwhile David Kearns, chair of the Xerox Corporation, has gone as far as to write a book on education: "As a businessman," he tells us, "I care about education, not for reasons of philanthropy and altruism alone—although they are important—but for bottom-line hardheaded reasons. I care about education because profits depend on it. Without it, our society will founder, and our businesses will, as well."

Kearns is just one of many business leaders worried that a decline in our schools could mean a devastating financial slide for America. Frank Shrontz, chair and chief executive officer of the Boeing Company, serves on Washington State's Blue Ribbon Council on Education Reform and Funding and is vice-chairman of President Bush's New American Schools Development Corporation. Boeing plans to spend 3.6 million dollars on kindergarten through twelfth grade education in 1992; it also endorses the principles for educational success established by the National Business Roundtable. Like Kearns, though, Shrontz is no mere idealist. "There is a growing awareness in the U.S.," he writes, "that providing our children with a world class education is not just desirable—it's a matter of our national survival as an economic superpower."

The major education reports of recent years—produced by government-appointed commissions that often include corporate executives—despairingly describe the state of schools and call loudly for their reform. Such well-known reports as *A Nation at Risk, Action for Excellence,* and *Making the Grade* all hinge on the hope that changes in curricula, structures, and methods will improve our position in the global economy. Some view education as an investment or a cost of doing business and call for its reform as a means of resolving our short-term economic problems. Their reports assert that strong public schools are the backbone of our ability to compete on the global stage: "If only to keep and improve on the slim competitive edge we still retain in world markets," *A Nation at Risk* warns, "we must rededicate ourselves to the reform of our educational system. . . ."

In the fifties business leaders called on the schools to help us win the Cold War—we needed more and better technicians and engineers, so the National Defense Education Act was passed to fund more and better science and math instruction. In the sixties and seventies the baby boomers went to work, flooding the labor market and depressing wages; the result was that business came to rely on sheer numbers to meet labor needs and to hold labor costs down. In this era business leaders were quiet about the schools; meanwhile the federal government scrambled to fund educational programs—vocational training and career education—that would confront the problem of unemployment. While the cause was worthy, these programs yielded a disturbing outcome: Labor markets became further saturated with relatively skilled workers who could be had at relatively low wages. In the end the labor intensive strategies of the era were profitable but shortsighted: while American corporations simply hired more workers, adding night and swing shifts to meet demand, the Japanese put capital into physical plant improvements and implemented efficiency and productivity programs in the long run far more effective. By the eighties their success had inspired American business leaders to find a voice regarding education again, this time with greater desperation than ever. The baby-boom labor pool had shrunk considerably, threatening to drive up wages and salaries, and furthermore their share of global markets was simultaneously diminishing. It was a time for national commissions and committees to make sober pronouncements and grandiose appeals and for business leaders to declare that our future economic health lay in the hands of our schools. Without more science and math instruction, they warned, more business courses and technical training, we would trail even farther behind our competitors. Business, in short, had come full circle: This was precisely what it had demanded in the aftermath of *Sputnik* three decades earlier.

Business leaders have long exerted a powerful influence not only over schools but over school reform as well, shaping through their roundtables, panels, and committees our educational vision. Most Americans share their desire for a healthy and stable economy, and because of this most have been willing to see educational matters their way: our schools as mechanisms for ensuring that business thrives in a combative world economy (one in which our competitors, we hear, make ruthless use of their own schools). Americans also do not want to risk that business will withdraw support from schools or that schools will not produce the sort of workers business requires. Their fear is fueled by the language of such reports as *A Nation at Risk*, which begins by speculating that "if an unfriendly foreign power had attempted to impose on America the mediocre educational performance that exists today, we might well have viewed it as an act of war."

It is in the context of all this that to most observers home-schooling seems particularly irrelevant. From their point of view it is institutional rigor that is required—longer school days, longer school years, more homework, greater strictness—in order for us to compete with the Japanese and Germans. After all, the Japanese go to school 243 days a year, the Germans 226, the South Koreans 220, Americans 180. Thus Massachusetts state legislator Michael J. Barrett has called for a 220-day school year, primarily on the assumption that this will increase our economic competitiveness. He points out that American students do less work and do it more poorly than children in many other countries. His antidote is forty more days each year of institutionalized schooling.

But Barrett's analysis ignores the point that our educational problems are rooted in the breakdown of families. It is abundantly clear that factors besides school-year length—foremost among them parental commitment to education—have enormous influence over educational results. Barrett's own data, published in the *Atlantic*, includes a chart entitled "Student Achievement by Subject Area," designed to indicate how poorly top American students do when stacked up against top students from other countries. Flemish Belgium students, among others, the chart shows, outperform their American counterparts in every listed category. Yet another of Barrett's charts indicates that Flemish Belgium students go to school 160 days a year—twenty fewer than Americans. Apparently the number of days spent in school is not the decisive factor, and such comparisons are mostly beside the point. Our economic health, it turns out, is not a function of how many days we go to school or even of how rigorous our schools are; what matters instead is the health of families, the commitment of families to education, and parental involvement in learning. This, not incidentally, is precisely what one finds in Japan or in any other country where economic vitality is predicated on educational success. It is what we find lacking when we examine the factors that influence education in our own country.

Despite the reams of evidence tying family commitment to educational success, business leaders pay mere lip service to the family while calling for reforms that undermine it. They promote schools as day-care centers servicing dawn to dusk their beleaguered employees, and when schools fall short they invent their own solutions such as on-site corporate schools. These schools ensure not only that workers can concentrate but that their children will receive an education consistent with corporate values and practices. Such schools allow parents noon visits to their children's classrooms and simplify daily transportation arrangements; carried to their logical extension, however, they complete the corporate quest for substantial influence over the content and manner of our children's learning.

That schools in their design have an economic function is obvious when we consider how schedules and clock-watching, regimentation and obedience, sensory deprivation and constant surveillance are the norm both in many schools and in many workplaces. Schools, say some historians, were designed from the outset—by the "visionaries" and industrialists behind the common-school movement—to parallel the conditions of factory life. Certainly it is no coincidence that state-controlled schools were born in the same era as the factory system in America: Industrialists understood the connection clearly. They needed to train a population of immigrants and of fiercely independent New World citizens to serve the needs of an industrial society.

Schools are supposed to teach critical-thinking skills in order to nurture citizens fully able to enter into a democratic society. Business, however, prefers an uncritical consumer society guaranteed to purchase its products. In fact, as John Goodlad's researchers found—a point made once before in this book—less than 2 percent of instructional time in many public schools is reserved for discussions requiring reasoning skills; Goodlad concludes that for the most part schools teach passivity. Yet even if we were systematically to change this, replacing the entrenched curriculum of passivity with a new, more democratic curriculum of independence—one that emphasized critical thinking—we would still find that in the case of schools, as elsewhere, the medium is the real message. For all our talk in the classroom of freedom, for every in-class critical-thinking exercise, there will always be a countervailing bell, a strict schedule demanding movement in herds, a dark background of authority, discipline, and regimentation that in the end constitute the truest lesson of schools and the truest preparation for modern economic life. "Think of the economic tragedy that would result if schools taught critical thinking," asks John Taylor Gatto. "Who would crave the mountains of junk our mass-production economy distributes? Who would eat the processed foods? Who would wear the plastic shoes? . . . How could the mass economy survive without the training 'schools' provide?"

Gatto calls the relationship between public schools and business "a strange symbiosis"; he describes the classrooms we put children in as "execution chambers," places where children lose their humanity to the needs of our economy. Hyperbole, perhaps, but for most of us there is a ring of truth to what he says, and we recall from experience our own sense of loss, our sense of living under the thumb of an inflexible institution that thwarted our attempts to become ourselves.

I am not asserting here that business is by definition a bad thing but rather that while schools may serve it well, they do not, always, serve *us* well. We are far better off thinking freely about matters and teaching our children to think freely about them; in the end that will sustain us far beyond the consumerism currently at the heart of our culture. Learning outside of schools might improve our grasp of what matters beyond purchasing goods and services: family, community, important work, service, respect for nature, dignity, morality. This, perhaps, is ultimately why we shouldn't expect business leaders to support homeschooling: It returns us to ourselves in a way that diminishes their control over who we are and what we do. It puts parents and children in charge of education, which is rightly where they should be.

Each fall I am impressed with how once again, business exploits the sales opportunity of the new school year. The back-to-school sales begin in early August, and parents are made to feel via advertisements the depth of their duty to buy their children new consumer goods before fall classes start. Corporate advertisers portray schools as stultifying places where teachers drone on about nothing that really matters to anyone, where what in fact matters most is how you look at your locker or to the boy who sits behind you in geometry, and where the true name of the game is, frankly, casual sex. Meanwhile, newspaper style sections run articles with such headlines as "Hot for School" over color photographs of fifteen-year-old girls in postures reminiscent of *Playboy*. "If looking smart ranks up there with being smart," kids are told, "the following belong on your back-to-school shopping list." They are then told precisely which products to buy: denim, Hypercolor, leggings, shorts, rayon sportswear, Swatch chrono, sweatshirts, Nike Air athletic shoes. Malls put out circulars devoted exclusively to back-to-school shopping, telling children where to get their hair styled, what sort of notebook is "in" this year, why teenage girls should carry breath mints in their purses beside exceptionally modest tampon containers. Adolescents are encouraged in television advertisements to buy hair gels, lipsticks, deodorants, and acne creams, candy bars that inspire Friday-night romances and sugared drinks symbolizing their membership in the correct crowd. Each autumn they bear this back-to-school barrage aimed at them literally wherever they turn: on the sides of buses, in the news sections of daily papers, on radio stations, in magazines, on television. The result is that advertisers come to control our children's sense of how to approach the whole idea of school: a fashion show, a social circus, a backdrop for superficial sexual escapades that are more about the ego than anything else, a place where what matters most is looking good. The blatant manner in which corporations broadcast to our young this damaging and irresponsible view of the world reveals their true position on education: The short-term, one-month profit each fall is more important to them than our serious educational problems.

Perhaps even worse are companies pretending a serious interest in educational problems in order to increase sales. "The West German school year is two months longer than ours," a Texas Instruments advertisement soberly reminds us. "As a result, the time our children spend in the classroom must be even more productive in order to compete in an increasingly competitive world. Which is why at Texas Instruments we are proud our tools for learning arithmetic and math. . . ." My complaint that such advertisements reinforce the use of sentence fragments is predictable—I'm an English teacher, after all—but I am more disturbed by the manipulative quality of such a sales pitch and the underlying hypocrisy behind it. The same is evident in Amway's salute to Dr. Henry Gaskins, an innovative educator in Washington, D.C., whom the company features in a two-page ad. Amway's point is that Dr. Gaskins—who is responsible for much good work among Washington's poor and disenfranchised—is most deserving of praise for educating a supply of loyal employees for Amway. "Some people are as reliable as sunrise," the ad copy beside Dr. Gaskins' photograph tells us. "You can see it in their smiles, feel it in their handshakes. You can tell their lives are fulfilling, their work rewarding. These are Amway people. . . ."

Perhaps it is true that what is good for Ford Motor Company is also good for America. On the other hand our national system of education should have loftier goals than to ensure that Ford's bottom line doesn't sink below Hyundai's. The ascendance of that goal among our educational priorities has succeeded mostly in hampering school reform that is visionary, long term, and successful. Finally, as long as the education of Americans is determined by the requirements of battle-scarred business interests we will have reform that is shortsighted, narrow, and designed chiefly to address economic problems in a stopgap, desperate fashion. Does business truly want productive employees, intelligent and creative people with a sense of responsibility and the integrity business requires? If so it should consider lending its support to programs that nurture the health of families and that cultivate in each family the value of education—far more laudable goals, it seems to me, than those business currently has for our schools and far more conducive to our economic welfare over the long run.

Most Americans, as Ned Hall asserts, are not much involved in their children's education, in part because the economics of their lives will not allow them to be. We might add that neither government nor business has done much to remedy this situation. It is a mainstay of our national debate about education to ask why parents have opted out, why they have deferred to educational professionals and assumed that schools will be responsible for everything. Educators complain about unsupportive parents who blame everybody and everything but themselves for the fact that their children are poorly educated; teachers decry career-track professionals with no time or interest in their children's learning and bemoan the fact that many of their charges come from homes where both parents, facing poverty, must work. Yet career-track parents are only doing what they've been taught to do by an educational system that prepared them for economic life while simultaneously excising them from their families; their absorption in self, work, and money are the inevitable products of our sociopathic schools, where they learned to compete for external rewards and to claw their way toward the top. Meanwhile, at the other end of the spectrum, the parents of poor children are at the mercy of an economic system that mostly precludes a life beyond their work. How can they cultivate learning in the home after long hours spent at dissatisfying jobs that consume almost every ounce of their psychological energy? (The salve they are offered is prime-time television, a perfect therapy for the day's illness.) It is unconscionable that in a country such as ours, so rich in resources of every sort, that vast numbers of people are condemned to working lives that preclude them from caring well for their children. They don't have time to do what parents have always instinctively done: cultivate their children's learning. And do we blame parents for no longer doing this when our schools have trained them, as children themselves, not to do it but instead to pursue economic success? Do we blame them when the economic facts of life have robbed them of the opportunity to do it?

To some extent, perhaps, the answer is yes: Parents *are* responsible. Those with the desire to take part in their children's education should stop waiting for the PTA to phone, asking them to purchase three dozen cookies for the next monthly meeting of the parents' auxiliary. They should stop wondering if the district subcommittee on community affairs or the administrative assistant to the superintendent intends to initiate an outreach program designed to bring parents into education. Such patient bewilderment and faith in the schools generally leads nowhere and produces procrastination; or as John McCormick writes in *Newsweek*, "both parents and teachers recite the timeworn mantra—'Parents and schools must work together'—and then blunder along separately."

Parents must also ask themselves exactly what they mean when they say they both *must* work full time. How much of what they really value are they giving up for a financial security that is, in fact, never really secure and for necessities that aren't so truly necessary? With some trepidation I point to this fact again: Most homeschooling parents earn humble incomes—somewhere between $20,000 and $30,000 annually—in order that they might teach their own. If this sounds to critics like self-righteousness, perhaps it is because they view purchasing power as the consummate good to be sought in life; those who give it up must be making a sacrifice in the name of some grandiose moral abstraction. The fact is that homeschooling parents are greedy and selfish—greedy for those things that give them satisfaction and for time with their children spent meaningfully. They have arranged their lives so that their homes are warm, their children fed and clothed, they have discretionary income for extras now and then, and on top of all these miracles we might easily take for granted they have time to spend at their children's sides while they learn what they need to know.

8

Before Schools

Anthropologists tend to view primitive people as *encultur-ated* but not *educated*—perhaps because they observe no schools among them. As difficult as it is to find an anthropologist who discusses education as education as he fleshes out his ethnology—religion, marriage customs, taboos, totems, tools, technologies, ceremonies, rites—many are painstakingly deliberate in their efforts to explain how their subjects are enculturated. The term generally signifies learning of the sort that expedites one's entry into culture: If you live by yourself (a feral child, say, rejected even by your wolf surrogate parents) and figure out on your own how to trap a trout in a small mountain pool, you are learning, yes, but there is nothing enculturating in it. Enculturation is instead the sort of learning that has a social meaning or cultural value—which includes, one would suppose, nearly everything we ever learn.

While anthropologists have failed to see education going forward among traditional peoples, missionaries have been less prone to this peculiar blindness. Precisely because their mission is to change things instead of merely to observe what is there they have generally felt that whatever the natives are doing—no matter how ambiguous or incomprehensible—it constitutes a kind of education. That is why, after building a church, missionaries build a school.

Schools, because they are abstract places where students look not at life itself but at symbols of life, texts about it, handouts, and reproductions, depend daily on written language. Every classroom has its blackboard, every class its textbook. Every student has a pencil and paper, and the first step in education is to learn to use them. Anthropologists will often use the term *preliterate* to describe people who have no written language, a term that suggests these people haven't arrived yet where we have as users of words. Preliterate may be construed as a historical term that defines a bona fide historical truth: Societies without written languages of any sort preceded societies that have them. Yet the term also suggests a value outside the realm of science; namely, that having a written language is superior to not having one, or that not having one is merely a step on the path to getting one. And where will "primitive people" get one? From us, of course, if history is any indicator. They will learn French or Spanish, English or Portuguese, and then they will no longer be preliterate.

Literacy is for modern peoples the unavoidable first step in education. We can hardly imagine an education going forward without the rudiments of literacy, and when we talk about education it is this image we conjure up: books, paper, pencils, words. Is it any wonder, then, that anthropologists fail to see education going on among preliterate peoples? That they see instead enculturation, an amorphous, effortless, and unconscious process?

While the language of anthropology might diminish its human subjects, we should nevertheless give anthropologists credit for avoiding an error to which less scientific observers have been prone. I am speaking, here, of the likes of Kevin Costner in

Dances with Wolves and of James Fenimore Cooper in *The Last of the Mohicans*, men who have indulged a large measure of romanticism in their portrayals of traditional peoples. In *Dances with Wolves* the Sioux never stoop to void their bowels the way white people do. The camera captures a light inside their tepees too brilliant, too inviting in summer and winter. When Costner's Sioux speak they are always politically correct about matters such as the plains and the sexes. Costner simply fails to report, as Erik Erikson does in *Childhood and Society*, that Sioux boys sometimes raped Sioux girls, who were taught by their mothers to tie their thighs together at night; that, in fact, "it was considered proper for a youth to rape any maiden whom he caught outside the areas defined for decent girls: a girl who did not know 'her place' was his legitimate prey, and he could boast of the deed." Erikson is faithfully reporting what his respondents tell him; Costner, on the other hand, has no reason to report faithfully and does not purport to be a scientist. His theme and purpose lie entirely elsewhere, and he seeks only to celebrate what was marvelous about the way the Sioux once lived.

Such glorification might serve for entertainment but does damage in the realm of education. Yet some homeschoolers are as prone to this romantic fallacy as Costner apparently has been. Inflating traditional peoples in the manner of Hollywood—instead of diminishing them in the manner of anthropologists—they arrive, ironically, at a similar conclusion: that traditional peoples learned effortlessly, unconsciously; that whatever learning occurred between their ears occurred as the result of some ambiguous osmosis; that in the Eden of the jungle no one was required to calculate, memorize, theorize, or analyze, apply a refined science or extend it. They conjure for their purposes certain satisfying dramatic images—a boy making arrowheads beside his squatting father, a girl watching silently as her mother weaves—and make of these a metaphor for the entirety of education among traditional peoples. Laboring under this romantic delusion they fail to recognize the sophistication of traditions developed over thousands of years. They fail to understand what traditional peoples did, and this ignorance colors what they themselves do when they homeschool their children.

I have known homeschooling parents whose primary educational theory is "that kids should be free, like little natives." They operate on the premise that in traditional cultures no one exerted themselves consciously or formally to provide children with an education. Successful emulation of this obscure tradition requires them to look on in detached amusement while their children "learn" from "being free like native kids": running about in a pack all day, chewing candy and trampling the organic-vegetable garden, hunkering down to watch cartoons whenever they feel like it. Adolescence converts this into adolescent terms: Cruising in cars, substance abuse, MTV addiction, and a yearning for video games are likely contemporary outcomes. Parents of these teenagers are often astounded at what the "traditional" methods have somehow wrought and are prone to conclude that traditional methods don't work given the facts of the modern era. When they have finally had enough of the results of their romanticism they put their children in school classrooms and toss their ideas about "natives" to the four winds.

There is, of course, a strand of truth in their naivete: Traditional peoples were far more apt to learn without teachers than we are and relied more than we do on "natural" processes: imitation, observation, absorption. Margaret Mead, our most well-known anthropologist, emphasized in *Continuities in Cultural Evolution* the importance to her subjects of "empathetic, imitative and identificatory learning . . . learning without intervention of a teacher." As a case in point Mead discusses the Cheyenne, who gave children bows and arrows at an early age and allowed them to camp on the prairie without adults as a means of practicing adult skills. Apparently one such group of children survived intact after a Cheyenne village was destroyed by enemies; the children simply went on with the way of life they had learned about from imitation and practice and re-established the Cheyenne community.

Accounts such as Mead's buttress the romantic's faith that children can learn mostly from unconscious absorption. So does John Honigmann's account of the Kaska, whom he describes as making almost no attempt to transmit even rudimentary information to their young. If a Kaskan girl tries to brew tea with cold water, an adult, says Honigmann, will let her go about it and refrain from pointing out that heat is required in order to make tea steep. Her failure to make tea might go unremarked upon even should she repeat this for days on end without any better results. She simply must learn on her own about hot water, and Kaskan adults simply trust that she will. In the end, Honigmann implies, she of course does.

Much learning did occur among traditional peoples via imitation, observation, absorption, and practice, but this fact should not prevent us from grasping the profound importance of formal training. Specialized knowledge—medicine, metallurgy, agriculture, ritual—was often transmitted explicitly and directly, and adolescent initiation rites most often included a formal teaching element. Chippewa children were lectured and counseled, and a boy on a vision quest received instruction from his father or from another man in his stead. Yoruba blacksmiths always learned from their fathers; Guarani children learned prayers by instruction, often at the hands of special teachers. Among the Nootka a novice learned the shaman's dance, its complex songs, gestures, and steps, from elderly relatives appointed to instruct him. The teaching was often intense and exhausting, for nonliterate peoples stored the whole of their traditions without written language, and this often meant many formal hours of word-for-word memorization. Among the Navaho, to cite one example, a cure for disease was performed by singers who memorized words, notes, gestures, and actions equivalent to the score for a Wagnerian opera—and did so without benefit of a manuscript. Yet it is one thing for us to be impressed or flabbergasted by the "primitive's" astounding feats of memory; it is another to acknowledge that formal education is part of many traditional cultures. Inasmuch as we might appreciate the informal character of much tribal education, we underestimate and devalue it when we refuse to acknowledge its many formal elements.

Most traditional peoples, in point of fact, educated with concern and care. They did not merely go about the business of life with confidence their young would learn by osmosis, nor did they isolate them in institutions where learning is divorced from living. Instead, responsibility for education was dispersed throughout the community and embedded in the daily life of all. Adults went about their tasks conscious of the presence and needs of the young and took time to explain, demonstrate, discuss, exhort, comment, correct, and answer questions. Chile's Araucanians, for example, urged their children to memorize tribal songs as a medium for transmitting the specifics of their culture; Arizona's Papago taught their young important rituals with great persistence and energy. Guarani boys were explicitly apprenticed to their fathers until, on the verge of adolescence, they received a series of formal counsels from the tribal elders whose task it was to initiate them into manhood. Meanwhile, Hottentot boys learned to play reed pipes from a tribal bandmaster. Among the Nupe, who were highly scientific farmers, a vast body of agricultural knowledge was passed down daily in the fields by older men, who pointed out mistakes to the younger ones and "scold[ed] boys for damaging a plant when weeding, or for planting seeds too close." A !Kung boy, at twelve, began to accompany his father, uncles, and older brothers on hunting trips, having passed his childhood listening at the campfire to dozens of hunts described in great detail. He learned from his father or grandfather to make snare lines and from his mother to identify roots worth digging from the ground. Among Florida's Seminole people the elderly were charged with the duty to teach the young proper conduct and correct behavior: "Education was in the home, learning by doing reinforced by the myths and legends which repeated the basic value system of the [Seminole] way of life. Girls learned the tasks of adult homemakers from observation and participation with their mothers and grandmothers in the matrilineal extended family. Boys learned hunting and farming skills from their fathers or maternal uncles. All this was reinforced by the myths and tales, told often by the grandmothers within the intimate family circle."

The Trukese are an excellent example of a people for whom family was at the center of learning. The methods and skills of hand-to-hand combat were passed from generation to generation of Trukese in intensive month-long training sessions closed to all but members of a single lineage. Similarly, a family's particular medicinal knowledge, as well as its lore and skill at magic, were transmitted in closely guarded family sessions that were halted in the presence of visitors. Trukese medicine men "usually reserve[d] full and complete knowledge of medicinal formulas and other lore for their own children. This point [was] so thoroughly accepted by Trukese that they consider it impossible for an individual to learn all another person knows about a spirit power, unless that other person is a parent."

The Chippewa, on the other hand, turned readily to sources outside the family when such was in the best interest of the child. Mothers taught their daughters to weave mats and build wigwams, make maple sugar and gather wild rice, but "if a woman had a reputation for tanning hides," as W. Inez Hilger explains in her study of the Chippewa, "a mother said to her young daughter, 'Go, learn from her.' " The elderly, too, played a significant role: A formal moral code was presented to boys and girls at puberty, "usually by the grandparents or, in their absence, by elders living in the community." They lectured and counseled, and children accompanied them at their work and in preparation for ceremonies and rituals. The elders told stories around the campfire with a view toward something larger than entertainment and felt responsible for the moral education of the young.

Traditional peoples used traditional methods for educating their children: direct transmission of skills and knowledge from parent to child in the context of daily living; moral and spiritual guidance from the elderly; apprenticeships and ritual teachings; storytelling and memorization; observation, imitation, and practice. Despite themselves anthropologists have gathered a great deal of evidence that education has often been systematic and that parents have always nurtured educational methods in sync with the rhythms of their lives. Nowhere is there evidence of parental deference to a caste of teaching professionals, or parental acquiescence to the notion that their children should live apart from them each day, cloistered from the world of adult affairs. This is exclusively a modern phenomenon, a recent experiment in both education and living.

Traditional peoples were first and foremost traditional; their methods for educating were honed and polished over tracts of time more vast than our historical time. We, on the other hand, are a new phenomenon in the garden of cultural occurrences. We owe it to ourselves to look closely, then, without either the anthropologist's or the romantic's brand of superiority, at the way traditional peoples educated their young. Our interest lies in a steady gaze at ourselves too, since we were not long ago them.

The anthropologist's distinction between enculturating and educating teaches us at least one important lesson about ourselves: We have divorced education from culture. We have created formal institutions of learning and in the process have excised learning from life, so that whatever happens outside schools is not generally thought of as education. We now have, in fact, two categories of learning: school education and the school of the streets—or the school of life, as some call it. When celebrities and authorities admonish us to get an education they are of course speaking exclusively of the former. The latter has become so entirely secondary that our language for describing it is at this point diminished: We can't even speak of learning in the world anymore without including in our notion of it the word *school*. "Make the world your school!" is a line even home*schoolers* end up using. For Americans schooling is synonymous with education; when we learn from living in the culture at large, something else is happening.

The grass-roots notion persists, though, that the school of life has much to teach, and it is common for our millionaires and corporate superstars (Ray Kroc of McDonald's is a good example) to glorify the education they received in the world outside of classrooms. This is because, in the ideological sense, Americans remain suspicious and skeptical about schools; they want to get rich "lighting out for the territories"—in Huck

Finn's phrase—and they still need the rich to wink at them and assure them lighting out is how it's done. Most Americans retain the historical instinct that says common sense is superior most of the time to formal school learning. They smile inwardly at those movies and television shows designed to reinforce what they already know: that good-looking country boys, trained in the woods, will always outsmart bespectacled yuppies who have had too much education for their own good. While this anti-intellectualism, so exhaustively critiqued, is of course inherently dangerous, we should learn to see it as a valid criticism of schools: They don't seem connected to *living*.

In fact, it is possible to point to a solid body of research—done by cognitive anthropologists, among others—that suggests school is divorced from life in serious and important ways. The president of the American Educational Research Association, Lauren Resnick, has gathered a number of studies underscoring this, including Jean Lave's 1977 look at tailoring apprenticeships in Liberia. Lave describes beginners watching masters at their craft before proceeding, quickly, to making garments of startling sophistication and complexity. "Although there is very little teaching," says Resnick, "—only occasional instructions or pointing out of errors by the masters—there is much learning through this . . . contextually embedded practice." In contrast, she points out, corporate America spends "at least forty billion dollars per year on educating and training its employees, mostly for managerial functions," yet "in corporate education programs people typically go to classes, take tests, and proceed through a sequence of school-like activities" rather than using "the workplace itself as a learning environment." They may master classroom situations, Resnick infers, without satisfying their employer's need for efficient, productive managers. Similarly, she points out, many military trainees "take theory-oriented courses that provide no hands-on experience with equipment" before moving on to "unstructured observation" and the kind of limited practice that "produces unsatisfactory results. Many trainees," adds Resnick, "never learn adequately, despite having mastered the classroom portion of instruction."

In separating learning from living, it seems, we have made education so abstract and artificial that it bears little connection to the world beyond schools. Many people will readily point out that they cannot remember what they learned in school, that the vast majority of what passed in their classes bears no relationship to their current life. Teachers are as apt as anybody else to be skeptical about their experiences as students: Most feel their college teacher-training programs were an absurd waste of time, hoops to be jumped through and little more; most acknowledge proudly that their real education came while on the job. In so doing they acknowledge a basic premise of homeschooling: that schools can temporarily prevent us from getting the education we persist in getting beyond their walls, where the conditions of life provide natural motivations and where learning is less abstract. "Never let your schooling get in the way of your education," Mark Twain purportedly advised. "The chief reason for going to school," Robert Frost said later, "is to get the impression fixed for life that there is a book side to everything."

Nonetheless many educators remain convinced that learning ought to be separate from life, that life in our culture is so shoddy and superficial, so banal and exploitive, that schools are somehow our last best hope, the last bastion of *real* culture against the relentless invasions of the tacky, commercial, and just plain idiotic. Without schools, they claim, young people would never learn that Emily Dickinson is superior to Janet Jackson or that Shakespeare is better than Vanilla Ice; they would grow up preferring "L.A. Law" to *Othello* and feel no uneasiness about it. Traditional people had this advantage over us: they did not have to worry that what their children absorbed through an education received informally, imitatively, would be *Teenage Mutant Ninja Turtles* or Arnold Schwarzenegger in *The Terminator*. Rather, they could transmit to their young a culture they believed in, while we must be deliberate and selective in our training, cultivating in our children the capacity to choose between the worthy and unworthy in our midst. How can this be done, the argument goes, without benefit of schools, which intentionally tune out MTV in favor of Milton, Dante, Shakespeare, and Homer, nurturing in our young our "best" traditions? (Even about these there is no longer agreement; the whole canon has been called into question after many years of blind acceptance.) Without schools, I'm told, our kids would have no counterpoint to *People* magazine.

It is a sad state of affairs when our institutions of learning can no longer proudly transmit our culture but instead are meant as an antidote to it (even sadder, of course, is how thoroughly they fail in this regard). Schools, like sand castles, cannot stem tides; they can only reflect like mirrors what is there—and a dysfunctional culture, or one that is diseased, cannot cure itself by looking in mirrors. If Shakespeare indeed matters more than Vanilla Ice, the proof must come from the culture itself, from communities and families, magazines and newspapers, television programming and cinema. Schools in themselves have not been convincing, and the argument that they are necessary to prevent cultural dissolution is given the lie by what we see around us. (Is Shakespeare on the cover of *People* magazine?) In schools students learn to live two lives: one in which Shakespeare matters so much that they must spend long hours writing essays on him, the other in which Shakespeare doesn't matter in the least and is rarely spoken about. The message is that our cultural traditions are the concern of people in a limited realm—schools—outside of which they don't matter at all and are of little interest. Instead there is the news that a singer named "Hammer" has a bone to pick with Sinead O'Connor or that a rock performer called Axl Rose is having problems with his neighbors yet again—one more bit of forgettable pop culture, served up to be chewed on between commercials, but certainly more central to our culture's shared life than an essay on *Richard II*.

If our culture is to be redeemed or salvaged—if the best is to be recognized by each succeeding generation as worth transmitting to the one that follows—then culture must have a life outside of classrooms, where fresh air can daily blow across it. It otherwise becomes stale, a curious artifact preserved in a museum; the vigor goes out of it in something of the way vigor abandons caged zoo animals. Culture—their own culture—is not something the young can study as though it were separate from the life they know, books living uneasily in an institution and unable to survive outside of it. Like those children we sometimes read or hear about who must pass life in plastic bubbles or expire, their precarious health threatened by the ordinary world's germs, culture is now trapped in institutions: museums, galleries, libraries, and finally schools, where children get their longest look at it. But the real culture, it turns out, is the one our children live every day: *Friday the Thirteenth*, Ozzy Osbourne chewing the head off a bat, Bo Jackson in a Pepsi advertisement, "Twin Peaks" one year, "The Simpsons" the next, the death of "Dallas" as a historical event, Disneyland, Madonna talking about group sex, Hulk Hogan, and Pee-wee Herman. We will not change this by insisting in school classrooms that what really matters is *Paradise Lost*. And we might even damage the health of "culture" further by incarcerating children in proximity to it and teaching them to associate *Paradise Lost* with boredom, dreariness, and the stale air of classrooms. Meet Culture, children; you'll be sharing your prison with him, while just outside his evil alter ego, Popular Culture, reigns supreme in the world of the living.

Our culture, it appears, is at odds with itself in more ways than just one. Hunter-gatherer and agrarian cultures were arranged so that one's satisfaction was derived not from personal or material success but from relationships between family members and between members of the tribe—linkages and ligatures to others. To be rich was to have a life in the web of one's people; to be poor was to have few children or to rarely see them or to work apart from those one loved. Industrialism and modernity have of course meant the latter; they have also inspired a need for mass schooling and altered the relationship between parents and children in the most fundamental ways. With industrialism, as Robert LeVine and Merry White suggest in *Human Conditions*, parents began to *provide for* their children as opposed to working, teaching, and living *with* them, and while they could no longer count on their children to provide in turn when the time came—emotionally, materially, psychologically, physically—they could at least derive some vicarious satisfaction from observing, distantly, the material and reproductive successes of their industrialized offspring. But this is a paltry substitute, in the end, for a life among one's people.

Mass schooling has had other ill effects, including the frustration and discontent that result, as LeVine and White tell us, when a society "awards certificates of failure to the great majority of people." Life at school is a pyramid, and while all believe they have a chance to reach the top, most are systematically eliminated by examinations and grades. Furthermore, the enormous competitive pressure placed on schoolchildren (and by extension on their families) inspires a variety of neuroses and anxieties. Children, of course, react against these pressures; their rebellion, delinquency, drug use, and identity crises are oft interpreted by psychologists and sociologists as likely responses to life at school.

More devastating, though, for modern people is the degree to which educational and occupational considerations have overwhelmed all else in life, including one's relationships to others. Our obsession with career now extends into early childhood, and our lives can be thought of as falling into three stages: preparation for, immersion in, and retirement from a career. "The members of contemporary industrial societies," LeVine and White write, ". . . have more of everything except relationships, and in the end these give life a meaning it cannot otherwise have." Traditional people, on the other hand, are immersed in family and community; part of this immersion, of course, is the living process of teaching and learning that all partake in and that all, ultimately, take satisfaction from.

We cannot be hunter-gatherers—most of us would not want to be—but we can, and should, learn from them. Our opportunities to learn grow when we refuse to either romanticize or underestimate how they lived. A society that embeds education in its processes, one in which parents, grandparents, friends, relatives, neighbors, and everybody else participates in the pleasures of educating the young, has the best chance not only to educate well but to provide for the satisfaction of individuals—and ultimately for the sustenance of what is best in its culture as well.

9

What We've Learned About How We Learn

The majority of homeschooling families are far better attuned than public schools to the revelations of *learning theory*—that subdivision of educational psychology devoted to discovering how people learn. Our schools, after all, were conceived 150 years ago, well before the advent of educational psychology, and have not changed fundamentally since then. Based on unexamined assumptions about the mind (or flagrantly ignoring what is known about it in the name of administrative efficiency) schools persist in the use of teaching methods both damaging and ineffective. They do not take seriously the central tenet of modern educational psychology—which is, significantly, the paramount premise of homeschooling too—that every human being pursues in a unique fashion the ways and means of an education.

That our educational institutions are so thoroughly at odds with what science tells us about how people learn should, at the very least, give us pause. The educational debate about choice, accountability, tracking, vouchers, teacher testing, cultural literacy, and everything else becomes secondary in the face of it. Such debate is ultimately more about tinkering than it is about the kind of fundamental change that would allow children to follow their singular paths as learners, and includes little talk about restructuring public education in the dramatic fashion learning theory requires.

Learning theory, however useful, contains within it a perplexing contradiction. Learning theorists would like to describe principles that govern the learning of many human beings—of all human beings, if possible—but their experiments and observations consistently produce the principle that every human being learns differently. Rather than elegantly explaining the facts (the way Newtonian mechanics explained the movements of celestial bodies), learning theory leads us to the paradoxical conclusion that no theory of learning is really possible. If learning theory were physics, every star would move differently, every planet would have its own complex strategy for spinning and hurling the way it does.

Inevitably, learning theorists disagree among themselves about almost everything except the notion that every learner is unique. B. F. Skinner and the behaviorists, for example, have amassed numerous facts about pigeons in boxes, rats in mazes, and people in laboratory settings. The best explanation for what they observe seems to them to be that both animals and humans learn by responding to stimuli and by getting specific kinds of reinforcement. Meanwhile Jean Piaget and his fellow cognitivists have asserted that learners do more than mechanically respond to stimuli and reinforcement: They carry within certain preexisting mental structures essential to understanding how learning happens. Piaget tells us that these structures develop predictably as children mature; stimulating and reinforcing behaviors of which they are not yet capable would be an exercise in educational futility. You can't teach an infant to do differential calculus even if you offer him his favorite animal crackers.

Cognitivism and behaviorism—the two main schools of thought about learning—are not entirely at loggerheads. Both underscore the unique nature of each learner, behaviorism by acknowledging that productive stimuli and reinforcers vary from individual to individual, cognitivism by recognizing the extreme importance of what the individual brings mentally to a given learning situation.

In fact, there is as much disagreement within the two camps as there is between them. The cognitivists in particular have disagreed with one another about such esoteric matters as *conceptualization, perceptual processes, correlative subsumption*, and *coding systems*, and about whether children learn best via *discovery* or *reception*. The terminology has not been particularly useful to anybody but learning theorists and professors of education; certainly teachers have not concerned themselves with it day to day in the classroom. The structure of school has prevented them, thus far, from putting educational psychology to work.

For discovery theorists such as the well-known Jerome Bruner, learning is an activity children naturally pursue so as to make sense of their world. Children, he tells us, are constantly about the business of forming mental categories into which they fit new bits of information; they busily create mental filing systems for related facts and experiences. The job of a school, Bruner's studies suggest, is not to present information systematically, prepackaged, but to require children to organize it themselves and to nurture their efforts to organize it. Bruner calls for much less in the way of traditional teacher direction and far more in the way of teacher guidance. He concludes that too little guidance will prevent a child from creating the mental categories necessary for organizing information; too much, he adds, will inhibit the child in the same manner. Teachers are left to discover the proper balance for each pupil and to find a way, given the crowds they confront each day, to do something meaningful with their understanding. Bruner tells us that we nurture learning by staying attentive from day to day—even from moment to moment—to each child's need for the proper level of educational guidance. While teachers find themselves in a poor position to do this, parents are extraordinarily well placed.

Bruner and the discovery theorists have also illuminated conditions that apparently pave the way for learning. It is significant that these conditions are unique to each learner, so unique, in fact, that in many cases classrooms can't provide them. Bruner also contends that the more one discovers information in a great variety of circumstances, the more likely one is to develop the inner categories required to organize that information. Yet life at school, which is for the most part generic and predictable, daily keeps many children from the great variety of circumstances they need to learn well.

Discovery theory clearly has profound implications for our schools, for it provides strong evidence that prior to kindergarten children develop not only powerful and personal learning strategies but highly singular methods for organizing what they learn, too. "Unfortunately," as Sylvia Farnham-Diggory, a Bruner protégée, writes, "the formal education system—based as it is on outdated, incorrect, oversimplified psychological principles—all too often collides catastrophically with children's natural learning skills, teaches them to mistrust and repress those skills, and moves countless numbers of children through 15,000 hours of systematic training in learning *not* to learn." Schoolchildren, she adds, "are trained to pay attention only to the very small set of cues emitted by the teacher, and to stop paying attention to almost everything else."

Harper Lee captures this in Chapter 2 of her widely read *To Kill a Mockingbird*: When Scout's first-grade teacher, Miss Caroline Fisher ("She looked and smelled like a peppermint drop"), discovers Scout to be literate, she looks at her "with more than faint distaste":

> Miss Caroline told me to tell my father not to teach me any more, it would interfere with my reading.
>
> "Teach me?" I said in surprise. "He hasn't taught me anything, Miss Caroline. Atticus ain't got time to teach me anything," I added when Miss Caroline smiled and shook her head. "Why, he's so tired when he gets home at night he just sits in the living room and reads."
>
> "If he didn't teach you, who did?" Miss Caroline asked good-naturedly. "Somebody did. You weren't born reading *The Mobile Register*."
>
> "Jem says I was. He read in a book where I was a Bullfinch instead of a Finch. Jem says my name's really Jean Louise Bullfinch, that I got swapped when I was born and I'm really a—"
>
> Miss Caroline apparently thought I was lying. "Let's not let our imaginations run away with us, dear," she said. "Now you tell your father not to teach you any more. It's best to begin reading with a fresh mind. You tell him I'll take over from here and try to undo the damage—"
>
> "Ma'am?"
>
> "Your father does not know how to teach. You can have a seat now."
>
> I mumbled that I was sorry and retired meditating upon my crime. I never deliberately learned to read, but

somehow I had been wallowing illicitly in the daily papers. In the long hours of church—was it there I learned?
I could not remember not being able to read hymns.
Now that I was compelled to think about it, reading
was something that just came to me, as learning to fasten
the seat of my union suit without looking around, or
achieving two bows from a snarl of shoelaces. I could
not remember when the lines above Atticus' moving
finger separated into words, but I had stared at them all
the evenings in my memory, listening to the news of the
day, Bills To Be Enacted into Laws, the diaries of Lo-
renzo Dow—anything Atticus happened to be reading
when I crawled into his lap every night.

Bruner and the discovery theorists have been opposed by a
second school of cognitivist thought that also has profound
implications for education, since it, too, points out the unique
nature of each learner. "Reception" or "assimilation" theory
finds a vocal champion in the educational psychologist David
Ausubel, whose work constitutes a thirty-year attempt to un-
cover the principles of meaningful classroom learning. Ausubel's
central premise is that meaningful learning—the kind in which
a learner connects new information to knowledge already well
organized in the brain—can and does result from the sort of
expository teaching we generally associate with the American
classroom (lecture, explanation, teacher-centered presentations)
as long as the exposition is firmly grounded in what students
already know. Ausubel posits that the brain accepts new information only if it bears connections to existing categories of
stored knowledge; if the new information is unfamiliar, alien,
the brain will find it meaningless and not incorporate it. The
duty of teachers, according to Ausubel, is to present information

in such a manner that students grasp the connection between it and the knowledge they bring with them to the classroom.

The promising new teaching technique advanced by Ausubel is really just the old-fashioned lecture with a twist: Teachers present information formally and verbally but begin by offering *advance organizers*—a complex of concepts introduced prior to the new material and meant to act as a bridge between what is known and the new things the teacher plans to talk about. The problem, says Ausubel, with our current teaching methods is that we too often lecture to children in a vacuum and expect them to perform a cognitive feat a good deal of research shows is improbable: learn material that bears no connection to what they already know.

For teachers Ausubel's ideas lend credibility to the notion that if one talks impressively and systematically, one's students are bound to learn something. But how can teachers possibly know what previous knowledge and categories each student brings to class? And how can they tune their lectures to what some already know without inevitably losing the rest? No wonder more than half of our students looked bored, distracted, irritable, or confused while we happily babble on about Shakespeare or Napoleon. Ausubel's theory predicts this.

In the end neither discovery nor reception theorists prove much of anything except that every learner is unique. In fact, no child conveniently bears out any theory or conforms to the model of learning put forward by any scientific camp. Nor does any child remain the same sort of learner year to year or even month to month. Thus public-school teachers must contend with the fact that no theory of learning can do them much good because the children before them are singular, complex, and ceaselessly changing, and there are anyway far more children in a given classroom than can be readily understood or significantly taught. Teachers must throw out theory and begin with the child, and this they cannot easily do in a rigid, overcrowded institution.

For some years now a group of "humanist" educators have attempted to turn schools into the kinds of places where the individual child comes first. What education ought to be about, they say, is gently helping young people to "discover themselves" and to pursue their own plans and interests. Represented in the early seventies by such education writers as George Dennison, Herbert Kohl, John Holt, and James Herndon, the humanist movement in education brought us the open classroom and the teacher as "facilitator," and emphasized the importance of the individual child's self-concept and personal values. It also failed in the conventional sense, producing students who could not compete academically with those from more traditional classrooms.

The humanists failed to educate well mostly because they ignored their own central tenet: The individual child comes first. They failed to provide the kind of structured learning some students need sometimes in order to thrive, and they assumed that self-actualization, self-development, intimate communication, and personal values were what all students needed from schools, to the neglect of other kinds of knowledge. They overlooked or dismissed the truth that children do need, each in their own way, to acquire thinking skills, analyze theories, and recall plain, hard facts. Finally, they stuck to the venue of the school classroom, where putting the individual child first is by definition highly improbable. Such humanist writers as Terry Borton and William Purkey espoused humanist classrooms in which humanist teachers did their utmost to overcome the unhumanist truth that large crowds of young people sat before them.

It has taken some time for the principle of individual learning to reemerge from under the shadow of humanist educators, who for the most part alienated Americans. In response to them we have seen a back-to-basics movement that ignores the truths of learning theory almost entirely in favor of teaching every child the same way: rigidly, in classrooms, and en masse. Its failure, too, is now self-evident; by almost any measure of educational success our schools are in desperate straits.

Perhaps the most talked about new theory of learning (the ideas of Skinner, Piaget, Bruner, and even Ausubel are today old hat to many educators) derives from work done by the Harvard Project on Human Potential and its codirector Howard Gardner. Gardner and his colleagues have amassed a substantial amount of research showing that human intelligence varies observably in type. Drawing on studies in genetics, neuroanatomy, neurophysiology, and neuropsychology, on profiles of idiot savants and prodigies, on cross-cultural research and biographical accounts of the variously brilliant and variously talented, Gardner puts forward a new view of intelligence with profound implications for our educational system; namely, that there are "several relatively autonomous human intellectual competences." Delineating the case for at least seven distinct *intelligences*—linguistic, logical, musical, spatial, bodily, inter- and intra-personal—Gardner challenges our traditional assumption that intelligence is something we can reliably measure by administering an IQ test.

Schools have long been guilty of promoting only certain intelligences—Gardner's linguistic and logical ones, the hallmarks of effective writers and scientists—at the expense of those students whose gifts incline them to grow in other directions. On the other hand, to suggest that schools remedy this by developing only a child's native talents implies a system in which we scientifically measure each child's potential for shot-putting, ballet, or nuclear physics, then train him or her accordingly. To Americans this is ideologically repulsive; our democratic instincts make us shudder at the thought of molding children this way. We prefer instead to expose them to a bit of everything and to allow them as young adults to choose their own path.

This preference of ours, ironically enough, is given short shrift in the real world of our schools, where children who are bodily or musically intelligent run up against a system with its own agenda. We may not be in the insidious business of doing what Gardner implies we ought to do—identifying early each child's "intellectual profile" and then acting on this portrait knowledge "to enhance that person's educational opportunities and options" (Newspeak for channeling children in the manner of the late Soviet Union)—but on the other hand our schools have not really allowed our children to decide for themselves where they are going. Schools instead encourage many in the belief that their own brands of intelligence—bodily, musical, intrapersonal—are relatively insignificant in the adult marketplace. These young people are likely never to find their own paths and to eventually turn their genius to pastimes or hobbies, pursuing livelihoods where they have no special gift and in the process doing no service to themselves or their society.

Yet schools continue to celebrate the primacy of logical and linguistic capabilities, since these are what our economy needs, and to discriminate against those millions of students whose special capabilities are otherwise. At their worst, schools function like Plato's sorting mills, culling out those who "can't think clearly"; inflexible bureaucracies, they cannot meet the needs of diverse learners striking out in various directions. School has no room for Gardner's varying intelligences or for the infinitely various ways of thinking we find among children; if students cannot "learn to think" (a recently popular buzz phrase among teachers, short for "learning to think like we do"), we mark poor grades against their names and toss them on the academic ash heap.

To suggest that there are many brands of intelligence is, as Gardner reminds us, nothing new; what is new is its scientific basis in systematic research. Schools must now contend with exhaustive evidence—not just humanist conjecture and insistence—that every child has a unique intelligence and singular potential. They will have to reconsider labeling as learning-disabled those children with extraordinary musical intelligence and rethink calling attention deficit disordered those whose bodies have their own peculiar genius (the bodily intelligent often suffer an Orwellian fate: They are drugged, with Ritalin, to ensure that their bodies' genius won't get in the **way** of what school wants for them). Our public-education system will have to be restructured so that each child's intelligence is systematically cultivated.

Those who advocate applying Gardner's theory to the classroom have, for the most part, failed to recognize that massive institutions are by definition incapable of such a sophisticated responsiveness to individual students. Proponents of this new vision have been extraordinarily naive about real-life matters, peddling, for example, the unwieldy notion that teachers transmit a given lesson in seven different ways: that they encourage musical children to learn to read by singing, bodily children by acting out words in pantomimes, mathematical children via computer software, intrapersonal children by going off alone to sit in quiet corners. In the real world such a classroom is a place where chaos reigns, not just because the logistics are so difficult but because thirty fourth graders do not fall into seven tidy intellectual camps—they fall into thirty camps instead.

Gardner acknowledges that this is so; in *Frames of Mind* he reminds us more than once that his seven categories exist in combination, are fluid, and "typically work in harmony," that their "autonomy may be invisible"—all ways of saying that no individual can be readily assigned an intelligence label (she's musical, he's logical, she's kinesthetic, he's interpersonal) without underestimating his or her complexity. He also encourages educators to pursue "the practice of matching the individual learner's profile to the materials and modes of instruction," which is, not incidentally, the central principle of homeschooling: Pay attention to the child's unique intelligence as it evolves and changes and adapt instruction and curriculum to it.

Unfortunately, Gardner ultimately undercuts his ideas by urging the educational planner or policymaker "not to lose sight of his overall educational agenda. . . . Individual profiles," concludes Gardner, "must be considered in the light of goals pursued by the wider society; and sometimes, in fact, individuals with gifts in certain directions must nonetheless be guided along other, less favored paths, simply because the needs of the culture are particularly urgent in that realm at that time." In other words, too many musicians don't help Ford Motor Company, so let's use schools to turn them instead into repressed but useful—if only moderately competent—automotive engineers.

I think of Caroline, a brilliant watercolorist, and her anguish about the C she received, after much effort, for her essay on Rudyard Kipling. I think of Lee, a voracious learner, who used to hide science-fiction novels in his notebook so that he could dream while I droned on. I think of the times I lectured on the connection between modern thinkers—Darwin, Freud, Marx, Einstein—and such modern writers as T. S. Eliot, Joseph Conrad, and Thomas Hardy. I would come away feeling certain that this had been a good day, a day on which everybody *had* to have learned because I had lectured so brilliantly, had held their attention from bell to bell, provided advance organizers and reviewed systematically, had, in short, done everything right, gone by the gospel according to Ausubel. Why was I surprised when, a few days later, half the class would answer incorrectly the simplest multiple-choice questions on the id and superego, natural selection, "The Hollow Men," and relativity theory? I had been a good teacher, but something, somewhere, had gone wrong anyway.

I think, in the same vein, of those classes in which I acted as *discovery guide* à la Bruner, nurturing students through self-selected activities designed to allow them their own revelations—oral histories, research projects, dramatic presentations, collaborative creative writing. Why was I surprised when three quarters of my students (students, remember, at a public high school with an excellent academic reputation) produced next to nothing or nothing at all, nothing of merit, nothing inspired? My surprise, it turns out, was a function of forgetting the central truth of learning theory: Each child learns differently. I had not been able as a teacher to provide for that, no matter how I might have tried.

The implications of all this are self-evident. Learning theory tells us to teach children as individuals who learn in their own unique manner. The finest possible curriculum is precisely the one that starts with each child's singular means of learning. Instruction and guidance are best provided by those with an intimate understanding of the individual child and a deep commitment to the child's education. These principles derive not merely from the homeschooling movement but from contemporary research into how children learn. They are not merely adages fabricated by homeschoolers but precepts grounded in a science that should inspire us to reconsider both our roles as parents and the shape of public education.

10

Schools and Families: A Proposal

Most of us now recognize, in one way or another, that our schools are not what we want them to be. In fact, we have been talking in desperate tones about schools for a good twenty years now, anxious that our debate yield reforms, and in that time we have asked interminable "commissions" to see to the restructuring of American education. They in turn have repeated the worn mantra—declining test scores, declining standards, more dropouts, more illiteracy—before delineating infinitely varied reform packages consistent chiefly in one regard: They give lip service to the fundamental role of families but promote reforms to which families are superfluous.

While most of our reformers have been unwilling to confront the matter surely at the heart of education—the commitment of families to the value of learning—they have attended to far lesser concerns: two and a half or three years of advanced math, 180 or 200 days of school, $25,000 or $30,000 salaries for teachers, more homework or less, more elective courses or more required ones, school choice or tax vouchers, tracking, magnet programs—anything but reforms aimed at nurturing families and cultivating them as purveyors of education. These latter

reforms perhaps seem to them improbable in a society to which
the family is now incidental, its force and value blunted by the
extraordinary conditions of modernity. Some reformers have
entirely capitulated to these conditions, acquiescing to the historical fate of families, and now espouse schools as full-service
institutions designed to do what families once did: Schools, they
assert, should be open dawn to dusk in every season of the year,
providing day care, meals, advice about birth control, counseling
for teenage alcoholics, sex education, AIDS education, late-
afternoon volleyball, basketball, and badminton, and finally
Home and Family Life courses in which children learn about—
what else?—the home and family life they have left behind.

These programs, however well-intentioned, work to pull the
final moorings out from under families, inserting government
institutions in their places instead of nurturing their fragile
health. They also unwittingly work to pull the last pins out from
under education, which, as we all know, works best when there
is family commitment to it. Educational reform, then, should
aim at strengthening the family instead of replacing it, which
means more than mere lip service to the family, more than
sloganeering at election time or sober rhetoric from government
commissions, more than inviting parents in for open house or
sending them the PTA newsletter. It means a thorough restructuring of our educational system, one that encourages parental
involvement, supports those parents who are already involved,
and energetically promotes the fundamental principle that education begins in the home.

While most school administrators have frowned on homeschoolers, viewing them by turns as a threat or an insult (but
always as a loss of potential state revenue), others have come
to see their promise and to grasp the importance of what they
do. Homeschoolers, for their part, have been far too inclined

to view administrators as their adversaries and schools as their enemies. Only in a handful of school districts across the nation—in San Diego, California; Sheffield, Massachusetts; and Kirkland, Washington, among other places—have public schools and the homeschoolers in their midst begun to cooperate happily. These districts are proving with innovative programs that schools and homeschools are not natural enemies but natural partners.

At first glance such programs seem incomprehensible: How can public schools provide a context for homeschooling when the two seem intrinsically at odds? To clarify matters we should begin by dispensing with the term *homeschooling* altogether, since it is both reductive and misleading. Homeschooling parents have as much zeal for pursuing education in the world as in the home; they see educational opportunities everywhere—in museums, libraries, art galleries, foundries, trout ponds, slaughterhouses, mountain meadows, and finally in public schools, whose administrators, they report, are sometimes more hostile toward them than the managers of chicken packaging plants or floral supply houses. Calling kids homeschoolers seems mostly a way to reduce, psychologically, their possibilities, to cut them off from the possibilities of public education, and finally to drive the wedge deeper between home and school, as if the two inherently preclude each other.

They don't, of course, nor should they. Families rightly should look to schools to assist them in meeting their educational needs, and schools should take seriously their constitutional mandates to provide for the education of every child— even the children of families who want to guide that education themselves. Homeschooling families desirous of help have thus far been left to fend for themselves and have felt the animosity of schools they support with tax dollars because administrators are upset by their withdrawal from classrooms or fail to understand their principles. At the same time, many such families have learned to see themselves as alienated from the notion of public education, have cultivated their libertarian impulses to the point of hysteria, and in thinking of themselves as homeschoolers have simultaneously reduced their sense of the possibilities of schools.

Public educators in some school districts have begun to take a critical look at the notion of an educational system universally applicable to all children. Faced with advances in learning theory and with the truth of varying learning styles, educators are now considering the value of offering a wide variety of educational opportunities. Some districts have instituted alternative programs that mostly attract those who, in one way or another, don't get along well in conventional schools; others have begun to see it as a duty to offer programs varying not only in educational content but in methods, structures, and guiding philosophies. Advocates of these programs have been opposed by staunch proponents of a nationwide curriculum (and by forces hoping to standardize education in order to achieve widespread cultural literacy) but have nonetheless pushed forward.

The Twin Ridges Elementary School District in North San Juan, California, is an excellent example of this kind of enlightened innovation. Thirteen years ago Twin Ridges instituted a home-study program that has successfully brought homeschoolers into the fold of public education, assisting them in their pursuit of family-centered learning and allowing them to make use of public-school resources and expertise. Twin Ridges provides homeschooling families with access to school libraries, computer labs, sports equipment and facilities, video supplies and curricula, workbooks, science kits, art supplies, maps, globes, and textbooks. Homeschooled children can take conventional school courses of particular interest or Tuesday-only courses designed specifically for them, and are welcome to attend school field trips and events: plays, musical performances, sporting events, dances. Meanwhile, the school district provides two home-study teachers for counseling, advice, and assistance to parents, who remain the primary educators. The home-study teachers also coordinate group activities, hold workshops for parents, run physical-education and music classes for children, and distribute a bimonthly newsletter informing families about upcoming educational opportunities: a visit to the Native American museum at Point Reyes, International Night at the Oak Tree Lodge, a trip to the Sacramento Symphony. The March 1991 newsletter, for example, tells families that over the next six weeks the district will offer workshops in "astronomy, botany, weather, rocks and fossils. . . . Please use these classes as a stepping stone for your studies and projects at home." Hours are given for the Oak Tree Library; for drama, quilting, and weaving classes; for workshops in dance, pottery glazing, shadow puppets, mapping, and geography. Families are informed about special events: a morning of roller skating at Sierra Skateland, an evening of stargazing in the school yard, a skit to be performed by homeschooled children, a Friday morning walk down the Independence Trail, a Thursday morning video production class. Finally, parents are told that the standardized tests taken by all second- through eighth-grade students in California will be administered to homeschoolers on a voluntary basis. "Last year Home Schoolers as a whole did very well on these tests," parents are reminded, "and the scores gave a strong, positive plug for Home Schooling."

Perhaps most exciting for school administrators is the news that such home-study programs often cost school districts nothing. In fact, home-study programs can increase district budgets by drawing in students who otherwise would not enroll, each of whom brings with him the same allotment of state funds—in some districts as much as $5,000—as students who attend conventional classes. The finances of such a program speak for themselves: 65 students × $5,000 = $325,000 in new state funds and involves the expense of hiring two certified coordinators (easily under $100,000) as well as resource materials, equipment, supplies, books, field trips, workshops, and contract services (also under $100,000), which means the program brings in substantial additional revenue (more than $125,000) for use in a school district's general budget. In Washington State districts are allotted about $3,000 per student, which means initiating a home-study program with 65 children would bring in $195,000—sufficient to cover the program's costs with perhaps a little left over. The financial principle at work is a novel and simple one in the bewildering world of educational economics: Children who primarily learn outside of schools require far less overhead. Twin Ridges' program, for example, is so cost efficient that the district is able to allot homeschooling parents a modest budget for ordering educational supplies; they can also borrow equipment from the home-study program's ample resource library.

Twin Ridges' success should inspire districts nationwide to initiate home-study programs. By encouraging more parents to teach their own children, such programs would not only help remedy classroom overcrowding and alleviate the enormous expense of building new schools, they would also help districts meet their responsibilities to diverse learners and diverse families. At the same time, such programs strengthen not only families but communities, encouraging everyone in the belief that education can and should happen beyond the walls of the school building. College students, the elderly, scientists, writers, assorted volunteers and benefactors all become involved as parents and home-study coordinators seek them out for their expertise and advice.

Notably, Twin Ridges' program has attracted the attention of families in nearby school districts—Nevada City, Grass Valley, Penn Valley, Pleasant Valley—which have since established their own programs. There are now five in a sixty-mile radius, accounting for more than two hundred children who generally score as well as or better than their classroom peers on state-administered standardized tests and whose families are now deeply involved in *public* educational matters.

Cooperative arrangements between school systems and committed parents, however beneficial and satisfactory to both, are sometimes constrained by state regulations that make them difficult to structure. While most states provide the regulatory means for public funding of "off-campus learning experiences," most homeschoolers remain wary of the conditions for enrollment placed on them by states. Washington, a state with relatively liberal regulations, requires off-campus programs to include a teaching component "including where and when teaching activities will be conducted by school district certificated staff"; it also requires that "student performance . . . be supervised, evaluated and recorded by the certificated staff or by qualified school-district employees under the direct supervision of the certificated staff." In other words, Washington homeschoolers who enroll in public-school home-study programs similar to the one operated by the Twin Ridges District will have to expect that *some* teaching, supervision, and evaluation will, by state regulation, become the province of the local district. How much of each is not specified, however, which gives local districts enormous latitude in determining the particulars of their program.

It is at the local level, then, that decisions about public school–homeschool cooperation must be made. The state of Washington, at least, does not stipulate how many hours of instruction from a certified teacher are necessary for students enrolled in such programs nor whether certified teachers must meet with students directly nor whether "supervision" means a daily, weekly, or annual meeting nor whether "evaluation" means a standardized test, a portfolio, or an informal end-of-the-year interview. Ultimately, nothing at the state level prevents a local district from formulating a home-study program acceptable to the various homeschoolers in its midst, one that places few if any bureaucratic demands on them and one that remains flexible and yielding to their varying sentiments regarding standardized tests, amount of direct supervision, administrative paperwork, "hours on task," and the necessity of reporting "learning objectives" and "outcomes" to somebody with a state certificate.

Local control over the specifics of public home-study programs is, of course, a double-edged sword: It means there is nothing to prevent a school district from operating a program so stringent and overregulated that homeschoolers see no advantage in taking part. The Seneca Valley School District, for example, in Zelienople, Pennsylvania, has elaborate procedures, guidelines, and regulations incorporated into its "In-Home Instruction Program" that for all intents and purposes prevent homeschooling families from pursuing their unique educational visions. Applicants must file a notarized affidavit with the district office outlining "proposed educational objectives by subject area," among other matters; they must then fill out an "Application for Home Instruction"—to be approved by the district superintendent—before attending a meeting with a building principal to review the family's "Home Instruction Program." The program, it turns out, is that of the classroom: 180 days or 900 hours of instruction per year in English, spelling, reading, writing, arithmetic, science, geography, history, civics, "regular and continuous instruction in the dangers and prevention of fires," health and physiology, physical education, music, and art. At the secondary level there are more requirements: four years of English, three years of mathematics, three years of science, four of social studies, two of "arts and humanities." The district provides each "in-home instructor/aide" with an "attendance register" for recording absences—a bureaucratic whim that speaks for itself. Seneca Valley "allows" parents to teach economics, biology, chemistry, foreign languages, even trigonometry—but only "at the discretion of the Home Education supervisor"; parents, furthermore, must have a high-school diploma (or equivalent) in order to participate in the program at all, despite all the evidence strongly suggesting that the level of parental education is irrelevant to homeschooling success. Finally, Seneca Valley requires participants in its "In-Home Instruction Program" to take standardized tests in grades 3, 5, and 8—tests administered by the school district, not the parents. It also requires that a portfolio of each child's work be reviewed annually by a building principal, an educational psychologist, and the district's director of special education. The results of all this elaborate evaluation are compiled by the assistant superintendent, then forwarded to the district superintendent, who—having nobody else to send them to—determines whether the homeschooling family at hand is in compliance with the regulations of the program. If not, an "impartial Hearing Examiner" is called in to "determine if there is an appropriate education. If it is determined that the 'Home Instruction Program' is not in compliance, the child must be enrolled in school and the parent will no longer be eligible to conduct a Home Education Program for that child."

In the name of consistency—as my father suggested to my

writing students—Seneca Valley should also stipulate that a child who fails in its regular classrooms "must be enrolled in a homeschool, and the classroom teacher will no longer be eligible to conduct a Conventional Education Program for that child."

Programs such as Seneca Valley's undermine the notion of cooperation between public schools and homeschoolers. Those homeschoolers who are all too ready to believe that school districts have insidious and totalitarian intentions have their suspicions confirmed when they hear of such programs; most conclude, perhaps rightly, that in creating them the schools simply hope to co-opt homeschooling altogether. In fact, many strong voices in the homeschooling movement object fiercely to cooperative programs on what might best be described as libertarian grounds: Independence, self-motivated activity, and freedom from government regulation are central to how they view themselves. They worry—legitimately—that the day might come when administrators and bureaucrats not only define what homeschooling is but dictate what homeschoolers do. They also point out precedents that seem to them appropriate: the women's movement, they say, was co-opted by corporate leaders, the natural-foods movement by General Mills, the environmental movement by Dow Chemical. Nothing is safe, these voices will argue, once government and business figure out how to exploit it, so the best policy is to go it alone, take no prisoners, and give no quarter to anyone.

It is not enough to point out in response that public home-study programs will always be voluntary and that laws protect the right to homeschool independently no matter what school districts implement. Meaningful environmental activism, after all, remains legal in a world in which the terms of environmentalism are now defined by business; a genuine feminist perspective remains legal in a world in which feminism now means power lunches; a grocer can legally sell organic oats at the end of an aisle filled with "All-Natural," "No-Preservative," "No Cholesterol" junk cereals packaged in colorful recycled cardboard. In other words, to co-opt and ultimately undermine a movement it is generally unnecessary to legally prohibit its activities; better to grasp and then exploit its appeal, systematically usurp its center, dictate the terms, define the territory, and relentlessly, if gently, push the early explorers to the side until in due time they become irrelevant. "Good-bye, Mom! See you at three-thirty! I'm catching the school bus to the Home Study Center!" And we close the book on homeschooling altogether and on the idea of family-centered education.

The Lake Washington School District, just outside of Seattle, has taken a novel approach to the homeschoolers in its midst that makes co-optation an irrelevant question. Lake Washington accepts no state funds for enrolling homeschoolers and does not bring them into an off-campus program like Twin Ridges'; instead it acknowledges fully and openly its legal obligations to homeschoolers in the district and goes one step farther by providing services to them *beyond* those required by law.

At the beginning of each school year the Lake Washington District contacts area families who have filled out a state-required Intent to Homeschool declaration. (In 1985 that meant 36 families and 60 children; by 1991 the numbers had nearly quadrupled to 135 and 236.) The district informs families of its legal obligation to provide them the opportunity for part-time enrollment and—at least as significant—for "ancillary services," including counseling, speech and hearing therapy, sports activities, testing, and remedial instruction. In point of fact, all school districts in Washington State are obligated by law to offer local homeschoolers precisely the same services they offer to other children, which means homeschoolers have the same right to computer labs, libraries, playground activities, text-books, cafeteria food, tutorial services, field trips, and specific classes (art, wood shop, and music, for example) as conventionally schooled children. Most districts, though, do not make it a point or policy, as Lake Washington does, to tell home-schoolers about their legal obligations to them nor do they invite homeschoolers to take advantage of the ample opportunities to which they are entitled by law and for which the state provides complete funding. An unexamined antagonism generally inspires school districts to either ignore or harass homeschoolers instead of serving them as required. Homeschoolers, after all, are taxpayers whose labors have helped to pay for public schools; as Americans they are entitled to make use of them.

Lake Washington—an exception to the rule—does more than merely acknowledge its legal responsibilities to the home-schoolers in its midst. The district, from its own pocket, has hired a liaison who is daily at the service of homeschooling families desiring professional assistance. On request, the liaison will counsel parents, help them select curriculum materials, teach homeschooled children, or assess their progress. The district also encourages its building principals to lend books or surplus curricular materials to homeschoolers in need of them and generally to help families address their educational problems. Significantly, the Lake Washington District places no demands on homeschoolers in return for accepting these various services; they maintain complete autonomy.

Lake Washington's program is unusual in that it operates as a financial burden to the school district, albeit a minimal one. Other districts accept substantial state funding for enrolling homeschoolers as "alternative school students" participating in "off-campus learning experiences," and therefore have greater obligations to homeschoolers *and* to state government, obligations that sometimes produce conflict. Both kinds of programs have substantial merits; neither is as good as it might be. They are in their various ways adequate to the needs of homeschooling families with their particularly strong commitment to education, but neither does much to encourage greater commitment from other kinds of families. Neither performs the essential task of educational restructuring, which is to nurture and cultivate learning in families where learning does not currently thrive and where learning must once again take root if we are to solve our grave educational problems.

In envisioning a restructured educational system we will have to take fully into account those external forces—social, economic, political, cultural—that preclude the utopian and the merely improbable, the seemingly outlandish as well as the impossible. If not, we risk the failures of earlier reformers, most notably those of the late sixties and early seventies, who saw educational restructuring as the foundation for a profound cultural change that wasn't about to happen. In formulating the education-driven Age of Aquarius these reformers dismissed certain American realities and as a result were summarily dismissed themselves as irrelevant to the mainstream of American life. They offered something neither palatable nor possible to the vast majority of their fellow citizens.

Perhaps the central fact of educational restructuring in our own time is that Americans *are* ready for certain fundamental, even drastic, changes. They are listening seriously to calls from a Republican administration for school choice, tax vouchers, and tax credits. They are entertaining the notion of yearlong schools after having held summer vacation sacred since Horace Mann's time. They are participating in a national debate about cultural literacy, multicultural curricula, declining test scores, declining standards, and declining literacy, among other matters. When they hear about educational experiments they applaud, and when politicians speak about dismantling our present system and replacing it with something entirely new, they find themselves more than merely ready to listen. They find themselves hoping that someone will follow through and do something—preferably soon.

In fact, calls for the restructuring of American education are currently more pervasive than they have ever been and seem to come from every direction. Libertarians and free-market theorists lobby for school choice and tax vouchers; cultural literacy advocates promote a nationwide curriculum, while multiculturalists promote curricular diversity. Educational conservatives call for revitalizing the old vision—more tests, more homework, more discipline, more required courses—while teachers' unions insist that "empowering" teachers is the solution to our educational problems. Corporate leaders want stricter academic standards and greater accountability from classroom educators; fundamentalists call for creationism, prayer in the schools, and a reassessment of "the humanist religion." Meanwhile, task forces, commissions, and blue-ribbon panels all have their say about educational matters: Most thoroughly deplore the present state of things and suggest an enormous variety of reforms. In short we don't know yet what we want, except that we want a lot of things, some of which are mutually exclusive.

In the sixties, despite a pervasive national sense that a lot of things were going sour, it was not readily apparent to the majority of Americans that their schools were lacking or ineffective. The reforms initiated by radical educators were promising and meaningful only to the reformers, who were unable to bring about widespread change, not because their ideas were ill considered but because they did not represent any sort of consensus about the problems of American education.

Today we have a consensus, of sorts—not about what sort of change we need but rather about the urgent need for change: Most Americans now agree that our current system needs an overhaul. This fact, however, does not give reformers carte blanche to institute changes that cut against the American grain or that do not take into account the realities of our time. The utopian adrenaline of the restructuring movement must be tempered by historical reason, economic wisdom, social understanding, and a soberly realistic view of the culture in which this restructuring must inevitably go forward. Without this sort of tempering we risk that—**as** in the sixties—notions of reform will lead to nothing and our schools will continue their disconcerting decline. Reform must be palatable.

My own first principle for education is that it ought to remain a *public* affair and a primary concern of governments. I am troubled by calls for privatization—the idea that education should be offered in the marketplace as a service regulated by market forces—because such a system readily lends itself to profiteers eager to exploit families out of greed. A nation of private schools will rapidly devolve into a nation of chain educational franchises offering McLearning in lieu of real learning, feathered out with slick advertisements and late-summer enrollment specials. Educational subsidiaries of major corporations will dictate not only what sort of schools we have but—even more disturbing—our very conception of the possibilities of education. We will lose, with time, our ability to discern the good.

Furthermore, schools as we currently know them should not be abandoned altogether. They have been in some cases demonstrably successful, providing well for the education of children bent natively in their direction. The option to attend a good public school of the sort currently operating in America should thus remain a possibility no matter what sort of restructuring comes to pass. They serve the needs of particular families well, so to dismantle them altogether would be to deny certain children an effective educational alternative. Within the limits of their possibilities, then, we should seek to make them as effective as possible for as many children as possible.

Yet I remain in disagreement with those who believe that in adjusting the schedule, rearranging the desks, opening a new computer lab, or otherwise tinkering we can meaningfully address our basic educational dilemmas. As long as schools remain institutions where hundreds, even thousands, are herded each day they cannot hope to work well for vast numbers of children. Schools must instead become extraordinarily flexible—public-service agencies offering a full spectrum of educational opportunities to the families they are mandated to serve. Thus it will be necessary to offer not only conventional schooling but many other alternatives on a sort of continuum; school districts will have to assist families in discovering the alternative right for them and encourage them to pursue it.

These alternatives should properly include, at one extreme, pure, unadulterated homeschooling of the sort my own family currently practices. This option is a viable one for certain families, producing demonstrable and extraordinary successes, and so should be promoted by schools. In fact, a school district should encourage *more* families to homeschool privately, without recourse to district resources—if families can do so with good results—since this frees the district to devote greater energy to those families truly in need of what it offers. Successful homeschooling, after all, is a kind of educational self-sufficiency, a farm that produces precisely what it needs without drawing on public funds. Such self-sufficiency should be promoted rather than mistrusted: It should be recognized as a legitimate and reasonable alternative to other educational possibilities.

Besides advocating private homeschooling as an option,

school districts should energetically promote public-school home-study programs. Like the Lake Washington School District they should provide free support services to area homeschoolers choosing not to enroll, and like Twin Ridges they should enroll those families who can benefit from home-study programs meant to assist them. Such programs should not demand any more of participants than state regulations demand of private homeschoolers; no added burden should be placed on them for enrolling in a district home-study program.

In most states, however—for better or worse—families homeschooling privately cannot do whatever they want. Washington, for example, requires homeschoolers to study certain subjects and to pass a certain number of educational hours annually; it requires parents to keep good records and to have their children annually assessed either via a standardized test or by a certified educator. A public-school home-study program requiring all of these things would require no more of homeschooling families than they are already bound to by state regulation. At the same time, a school district should honor its responsibilities to homeschoolers after collecting funds for enrolling them. Its program, by regulation, must include "teaching activities" offered by "school district certificated staff"—which means, for example, special courses for children, workshops for parents, seminars for families, tutorial sessions, and access to conventional school classes and activities. A district also cannot collect state funds unless it employs a staff member to supervise, evaluate, and record the progress of participating home-study students. These efforts can be interpreted by homeschooling families as an imposition on the part of a school district; they might also be interpreted as services, however, that correspond precisely to what families are required to do—by state regulation—should they choose to homeschool privately.

Understandably, many homeschooling parents would prefer

to supervise, evaluate, and record the progress of their children without assistance from their local school district. This is certain to be the case where districts do not take parents seriously or allow them to act in a primary role as educators of their children. The success of a public-school home-study program, then, comes down to a district's willingness to cooperate in a meaningful way with homeschoolers. This implies a fundamental shift in educational philosophy and a commitment to parents who wish to take primary responsibility for educating their children, with school systems in essentially supportive roles rather than the other way around. Such a philosophical position should be central to the stated objectives of any public-school home-study program, the core of its reason for being.

An ideal program would offer all the services that I have described as available in Twin Ridges. It would employ a home-study coordinator (salaried via state funding that accrues from increased enrollment) to organize workshops for parents and children, directly tutor and teach when requested, schedule field trips and community events, direct home-study families to community and school resources (the coordinator could keep a compendium of local educational resources, with names, phone numbers, and services offered by members of the community), arrange work-study programs and apprenticeships, locate materials and texts for students, assist collaborations between home-study families, contract private educational services for them and provide information about available activities (Twin Ridges' newsletter is a good example), and finally cultivate— even design and create—educational opportunity in the community at large.

A good program would include a yearly budget for family purchases of educational materials (to be made through the program coordinator), recreational and social activities designed specifically for home-study children, opportunities for home-study children to participate to any degree desired in conventional school classes and extracurricular activities, and a library or resource center filled with curricula, supplies, software, lab equipment, educational videos, workbooks, and texts all available to home-study families on a check-out basis.

While it is important for school districts to take seriously their obligation to provide fully for the educational needs of homeschoolers, it is even more important that they encourage greater commitment to education on the part of *schooling* families. Districts should offer ongoing evening seminars designed to promote this sort of commitment and to inspire in more parents a greater involvement in the education of their children. Workshops should be offered to parents uncertain of their teaching abilities. (Local homeschooling parents might illuminate in these workshops their successes and failures, reflect on their educational tribulations, discuss various educational methods, and in general provide the kinds of insight gained from home-schooling experience.) A district newsletter should keep parents abreast not only of workshops and seminars but of the spectrum of educational opportunities available to their children, reminding families often of the possibilities in the district beyond conventional schooling. Families should be encouraged to find their proper relationship to schools, selecting a degree of parental involvement appropriate not only to their finances and schedules but to their values and educational philosophies as well. For those desiring it conventional schooling should be available; others should be able to choose the degree of involvement and the kind of services they want from their local school district. Meanwhile, as a matter of policy the district should persist in encouraging families to take the lead in formulating an education for themselves and to view the school district as a government agency providing assistance, resources, expertise, opportunity, and most of all support for the idea that education begins in the home.

I can imagine that many parents would choose to change nothing, that finding their children's schools satisfactory they would see no need for change. I can imagine that others would continue to press for changes that would make schools more satisfactory to them, and I would applaud their efforts. Yet I can also imagine families deciding on new arrangements—perhaps sending a child to school part time for wood shop, history, and algebra but seeing to other matters through their own efforts and through the district home-study program's resources. Perhaps some children would attend field trips and assemblies, play on sports teams and write for the school paper, take part in student government and the activities of the French Club but take no academic courses at the school, preferring to pursue academic matters on their own and at home. Others might take vocational education courses designed to teach construction skills; earn work-study credits while working as journeyman carpenters; apprentice themselves to local architects, surveyors, or engineers; take advanced algebra at the local high school but study other subjects at home. Still others might never enter school classrooms, instead counting on the district's home-study program to assist them in finding community resources: the marine scientist willing to clean a salmon stream with them, the farmer who will show them how to raise and breed chickens, the county library's reading series and the county hospital's health seminars, the retired English teacher at the convalescent center eager to tutor young people. As families become more enthusiastic and confident the novel arrangements and idiosyncratic strategies will proliferate, as well they should, for the best education is the one formulated and designed to meet the novel and idiosyncratic needs of individual children.

Bureaucratic inertia, fear of complications, worries about college credits, and assorted "administrivia" should all be dismissed as considerations that might prevent a district from instituting such a program. These considerations—which are just more anxiety about efficiency, about losing control over educational processes (education on the factory model, as though we were producing cars or widgets instead of serving young human beings)—have for too long now prevented us from making educational progress. The central question of restructuring should not be whether school administrators have the energy to create a new kind of educational system dedicated to a new vision. Taxpayers should take it as a given that administrators—honor-bound and dedicated professionals—will concern themselves far more with creating the best possible system than with whether or not reform will upset the administrative status quo. We should rightly fear that educational progress might be subverted by the inherent inertia of a comfortable bureaucracy unwilling to confront the demands of change.

But in the end restructuring is more about families than it is about schools, home-study programs, or administrators. Our educational problems exist because the American family is in disarray, buffeted by forces beyond its control that have made it far less effective than it once was as an agent of education. So while local school districts might restructure in such a manner as to promote education in every home and to assist every family in its effort to educate, families, too, must look at themselves and ponder their commitments and values. We all must examine how we live and what we live for and whether some of our educational problems derive not so much from schools as from ourselves. Rather than waiting for restructuring to happen— rather than expecting that some miraculous change in the way professionals organize schools will solve all our educational problems one day—we will all have to look inward. We will have to stop blaming schools alone for the educational mess we have got ourselves into. We will have to find in ourselves the will to overcome the historical and cultural forces that have thus far prevented us from seeing successfully to education. The schools, ultimately, might restructure, but it will do us no good unless we change who we are and what we do.

11

A Life's Work

If homeschooling means foremost teaching one's own, it also means answering questions about it put by friends, relatives, even strangers. In the face of this homeschoolers—including myself—have learned to be far too often defensive, for we consistently find ourselves interrogated at length when the subject of homeschooling is broached. It should be easy to understand how friendly conversation in America—where probing into the particulars of other lives is considered courtesy ("Always ask about *their* lives" is the advice we get as teenagers about making polite talk)—can lead swiftly to an inquisition on homeschooling. What's your name? Where do you live? What do you do for work? is inevitably followed by: Do you have children? How many? How old? Boys or girls? What grade are they in? Which school do they go to?

When it turns out the children in question go to no school at all, the line of inquiry turns. A few of my inquisitors have simply lost the beat altogether, stumbling over this unexpected bit of information the way one stumbles over an exposed root in otherwise harmless terrain. Homeschooling? What? That can't work, can it? Isn't it mostly fanatics? Shortly they begin the awkward work of apologizing for their recklessness, conducting themselves as though, having made a Polish joke or two, they suddenly discover I'm from Warsaw. Despite all my ready assurances—no insult taken—they often turn up the sensitivity meter a few notches in preparation for conversation on a higher plane.

But this, of course, is only one twist talk can take, the interstices of which, while uncomfortable, are rarely unfriendly. I have met, too, with drunken confrontationalists, itinerant educational philosophers, and closet talk-show hosts posing as party guests. I have answered the polite questions of the cleverly deferential, discreet surgeons who have **a** way of metamorphosing late in the game into highly skilled cross-examining prosecutors. I have responded to the agreeable and the curmudgeonly, the sore at heart and the too often abused, the politically correct dentist and the unapologetic fascist, the merely confused, the badly battered; to the insurance agent working his beat, wary not to tread on my toes lest I opt against purchasing a whole life policy; to the weary physician making amiable conversation while tapping at my chest or shining light up my nose; to the meekest, most neutral information gatherers of the world who are merely storing everything away out of habit or because they believe it might come in handy. I have spoken with all of them, and what I have noted over the years is not bitterness or anger or enmity so much as the fact that homeschooling interests each—or rather the particulars of my homeschooling life interests each, for it is not theirs and remains mysterious. What made you want to teach your own? they ask. What leads a man to it in the first place?

This *man* notion, to begin with, is often critical. For I have faced more than once a brand of suspicious interrogation designed to establish that I do not homeschool at all, that my wife does the job of homeschooling our kids while I, on the other hand, merely talk about it. After all, I am a schoolteacher, she doesn't "work," she's home, I'm not, and so on in this vein—until my antagonist begins to nod in a manner I've come to recognize. By merely answering their questions (yes, I work outside the home; no, my wife doesn't) I confirm their opinion that homeschooling is sexist, that its most obvious result is the isolation of women in homes, away from the fulfillments of the workplace. (That there may be fulfillments in the home for both sexes as educators of children is another issue.) I sooner or later hear myself say that the question of who does what in a relationship is no more or less important with regard to homeschooling than it is with regard to anything else: who does the dishes, changes the oil in the car, shops for food, flies to Miami on a business trip. The question of *who does what* remains: who takes responsibility for the child's introduction to long division, drives him to swimming lessons, teaches her to throw a baseball, shows her how to use a calculator. Homeschooling, I point out, is no more inherently sexist than anything else in a marriage, and if in many homeschooling families the mother is the prime mover and first cause of education and the father an addendum and auxiliary, this is a reflection on the culture at large and not on the phenomenon of homeschooling.

Yet even this is tangential, really, to the stream of curiosity I have paddled against. The sexism question is an eddy, it seems for most of my interlocutors, and the main current lies elsewhere among their questions, having more to do with why I homeschool than with if I do or if my wife does. Once we are past the basic questions—academics, socialization, legality, elitism, sexism—it turns out that the heart of the matter, the part that holds heat, is this question of how I have chosen to live, why I have chosen to be this way: a teacher to my own children.

The centrality of that should tell us something. Bankers, lawyers, store clerks, poets, accountants, engineers, loggers, graduate students—the majority would rather know about me than my children, are more interested in life-style than education, would prefer hearing about the arrangement of my day, not curricula and methodology. My children are only momentarily a part of most homeschooling conversations in which I've engaged; after that the spotlight moves to me. I am sometimes dismissed as a crank or eccentric, an innocuous moralist or wrongheaded idealist, even as an outright fanatic. Whatever and however the case may be, few of my questioners want to talk about education. Of those who do, some repeat what they have read in newspapers, soberly pessimistic, gravely factual, spicing their epiphanies with local anecdotes: the kindergarten teacher at the nearby elementary who verbally abused the daughter of a friend, a neighbor's experience on the curriculum restructuring committee with a district administrator pushing whole language theory, a son's fruitless attempt to initiate an independent-study project on frogs with his high school biology teacher. But most simply don't want to talk about education in even a cursory way. What they are interested in, instead, is my daily schedule; they want to know how it's possible for someone to earn a living *and* to educate his kids at home, and they suspect that probably I don't in fact do both. Either I'm independently wealthy or I leave all the homeschooling work to my wife or I have no life beyond my job and wearisome homeschooling labors (this is the favored hypothesis of the earnestlessly sympathetic) or—a last-resort theory—my kids simply aren't getting educated.

I have noticed, too, that many of my interlocutors—men, particularly, far more than women—have a propensity to explain at length and in detail how the nature of their jobs, the texture of their days, the sheer difficulty of working and commuting—how all of this prevents them from homeschooling. They speak of me, at this point, as "lucky," "fortunate," "unusual," and they very often say something to the effect that while in certain regards they find homeschooling attractive the tenor of their lives precludes it. "For most people it isn't possible." "Even if I decided I wanted to do it there wouldn't be the time or energy." "Look, while you and your kids are taking nature walks, I'm stuck in traffic on the bridge somewhere with my briefcase open, writing memos."

Like Nick Carraway in *The Great Gatsby*—a novel I read year after year with junior and senior literature students—I have been subject to the private griefs of men, not because I pass no judgments but because I homeschool. Men have opened their hearts to me upon hearing that I teach my children and take pleasure in it (the latter is variously construed by some as artless guile, innocuous fluff, or of dubious sincerity). Some claim to want to live as they imagine I do and will often regret aloud their manner of being, at times with a vociferous, even bellicose frustration, at times humbly and wistfully. However it may be, it is significant to me. I come away impressed with how deeply the will to teach one's own is imprinted on the human spirit.

Week after week in 1991 we saw Robert Bly's book *Iron John* at the top of national best-sellers lists. Already, of course, the backlash has occurred, and it has swiftly become fashionable in certain quarters to ridicule the men's movement and to dismiss Bly as a heavyweight poet gone fuzzy and popular—pop schlock with a *Myths to Live By* spin, Robert Fulghum with the brain of Carl Jung. Meanwhile the men's movement, at the mercy of forces outside its control, has by now been reduced in the public eye to a convenient set of belittling images: Bly in his incomprehensible sweater vest, looking mystic; half-naked accountants on weekend retreats howling their grief at the forest moon; latter-day warriors wearing bifocals and sandals, squatting by fires to temper spears they have lovingly devised, and so forth *ad nauseam.* Throw in, for good measure, Bill Moyers' earnest questions, Bly chanting cryptic answers in the form of poetic metaphors, and you have the recipe for a "Saturday Night Live" skit.

Anything dangerous, anything like a movement of men (which might change America as thoroughly as the women's movement has changed it), must be dealt with summarily and without a hint of mercy lest it threaten the kingdom built here. The style and ritual of the men's movement may lend itself to ridicule, is often absurd, fatuous, even comic, but that should not prevent us from giving serious thought to its more profound aspects. Imagine men deciding, en masse and angrily, that their true interest, their real fulfillment, lies not in the halls and offices of corporations but in the lives of their families, in the lives of their wives and children, brothers and sisters, friends and neighbors, in the lives of their parents as they grow old and in the life of the communities they inhabit. Imagine men discovering that their frustration and unhappiness has everything to do with the nature of their work and the thinness of the connection between themselves and others. Such an enlightenment would weigh heavily on the status quo in this country, where an entire culture is ill and confused in large part because men have no true place in their homes any longer and haven't for more than a century. They leave in the morning, return at night, and the great chasm between—men report this emptiness—becomes inexorably a part of them.

So there are perhaps reasons why, in conversation with men, I hear my interlocutors compelled far more strongly toward talk of how I arrange my life than toward talk of homeschooling's particulars. For some it is an opportunity for a vicarious fantasy; having indulged it, through me, however fleetingly, they can go on with lives they themselves have characterized as quietly desperate, unacceptably and undefinably lacking. For others it is important to dismiss me, since I threaten them as somebody who, to their way of thinking, has chosen family over work (as though the two were mutually exclusive). For reasons such as these, homeschooling conversations are usually heavily freighted with silences and euphemisms; they are about values and thus electrified by nervous tensions, animated either by strained politeness or bitterness and gall.

Often, in fact, the mere mention that I homeschool is taken as a sort of indictment of my listener, as if my point in bringing it up at all—in answering a query about where my kids go to school—is that my homeschooling makes me morally superior. The assumption is that I am sacrificing something, enduring an extreme hardship, cultivating selflessness and performing well as a father under duress in order to meet my ethical standards about the education of my children. By extension I must be condemning others for their selfishness, for every time they have chosen golf with friends over a trip with the family to the museum. Those who make especially good livings, who can afford many luxuries and exotic vacations, are especially vulnerable to this sort of delusion; guilt (and pain) at toiling long hours for money, far removed from the heart of family life, drives them to make something out of nothing, maybe. It is interesting to me that the well-heeled and long toiling are far more likely than anybody else to call themselves firm believers in the public schools as the surest foundation for democracy and to insist that they send their children to them because they believe in a democratic society. Feeling morally condemned, I suppose, they make a point of returning the favor. They do not want to feel that homeschooling is, in effect, a challenge to the authority of their worldview.

Rarely am I able to convince these men that homeschooling

only sometimes feels like hardship. If I say it is far more often a source of satisfaction, the statement is again construed as a sign of a carefully concocted moral superiority: *Oh, I don't mind hauling water all day, it is simple and beautiful, part of my way along the path,* delivered with a beatific smile. Later in the conversation they will seek to pin me down about what I do, how many formal desk hours I pass at my children's sides, a textbook before us, a work sheet at hand—and if I am consistent in this regard, if I am up out of bed at a decent hour, following a regimen, progressing through algebra, systematically covering the Civil War, if I am disciplined, focused, genuine, if I am actually hauling water or merely talking about it. If not then of course no hardship is involved—I'm merely depriving my children of a real education in the name of bizarre philosophical principles.

While informal discussions of homeschooling range wide, poking into private corners one moment, taking on humanity's deepest questions the next—how we know anything, how we see the world: ersatz epistemology or phenomenology—most "professional" discussions of the subject (the ones engaged in by state-certified educators) are predictably limited in scope and nature. They focus on learner outcomes and learning theory, examination procedures and legal constraints, curriculum development and methods of pedagogy—important matters, but nonetheless limited ones, too. The rare professional dialogue about home education in the larger context of social dilemmas is less limited, less technical, but often more abstract and less immediately useful; it doesn't lead to any concrete *change* and is thus engaged in at best halfheartedly and at odd moments, in a piecemeal fashion. Can we blame teachers for being like this? I, too, have passed long hours listening to windy educational rhetoric, locked into highly theoretical conversations, suffering while eloquent and passionate people discourse at length among the clouds, and have afterward pondered with colleagues in the parking lot whether anything said, anything written down, will make any difference tomorrow in the classroom or for that matter at any time ever. Many teachers I know live perpetually with the sinking feeling that the answer is always and forever no, and these people, often peppy extroverts in the classroom, suffer from a chronic, painful cynicism about the real possibilities of their profession. Some exhibit a neurotic eagerness, a workaholic rabidness as an antidote to pain, insisting by the force of their personalities, their strained faces, that self-sacrifice can indeed make a difference in institutions they recognize as fatally flawed; others go sullen and silent about everything, dividing themselves psychologically into two distinct people, one who teaches in order to pull a wage down, another who has an alternate life of compensatory hobbies, down-in-the-mouth skepticism, and sweet, summer-season fantasies. Teachers are more likely than anyone else to altogether avoid the subject of homeschooling, not because they are philosophically opposed but because they are exhausted with discussions about education that lead nowhere and produce nothing. They are too busy confronting the psychological dilemma of meeting, tomorrow, 150 students and have only small reserves left over for abstract dialogue.

Yet I admire the teachers at my high school. Most are in it for the right reasons. Most are driven to fulfill their obligations by nothing more complicated than a keen sense of right and wrong and by a feeling of communal responsibility. But most are also troubled people, forever battling the institution they serve, manacled to it, out of sync with it—prisoners lashed to a cart. They are always hopeful that next year things will begin to go right, that down the road a little their voices will be heard;

either that or they soon cease speaking, cease hoping for anything in particular. In either case they have come to their profession as if driven by an instinct, and there is something in each
of them—no matter how surly, burned-out, or disenchanted on
the surface—that compels them to share with young people
some part of things, some area of life they know about. I admire
them not for this precisely but more because they have refused
to ignore that inner voice prompting them to teach.

This teaching voice gathers in every parent. Often dismissed,
often ignored, but more often persisting and welling up at odd
moments—in kitchens, theaters, and in the waiting rooms of
hospitals, in airports and train stations, in dentists' offices and
at museums, on fishing trips and in the middle of long automobile journeys, at funerals and parades, and while riding in
subway cars—in all these places the voice of the parent is heard
pressing forward in spite of everything. Ordinary people have
always been teachers; it is only recently that teaching has become
a salaried profession instead of a part of daily existence.

The gap and discomfort in modern life, the anxiety most
feel, the sense of being troubled—the modern condition, as my
students learn to call it—has been exhaustively discussed and
exhaustively written about, so that by now the concept is as
weary as a character in a play by Jean-Paul Sartre. Psychologists,
anthropologists, philosophers, novelists, poets, metaphysicians,
and intellectual historians have all sought to document its
sources and symptoms by touching on the death of God, the
birth of the bomb, Darwin's finches, Freud's id and superego,
the theory of the big bang, existential angst, entropy, the death
of stars. Industrialization, nationalism, world war, and population growth have also been named as co-conspirators in the
death of humanity's peace of mind. Poets describe it another
way: Ripped from the long-hallowed womb of place, from the

mountains, deserts, valleys, and living plains and from the bosom of home and community, we no longer know where we are in relationship to anything else in the world. Cut off and surrounded by an abyss we starve in silence. Parched by thirst we recognize nothing but thirst and possible signs of water.

The nature poets tell us that we have traded for modernity our tranquil place on the planet. Word has it that in return for central heating and automobiles Mother Earth has exacted a price we can't afford: emotional disequilibrium, psychological turmoil, cultural strain and disruption. But by now our deepest thinkers mostly agree that there isn't going to be any turning back—the feral people of the radical environmental movement, even they drink Pepsis. We will not again be tribal peoples.

We can waver indecisively in our conclusions about dead cultures, pondering whether New Guinea's headhunters were remorseless homicidal maniacs—psychotics with bad teeth and voodoo dolls—or whole, satisfied, "in touch" *Natürvolk*—but such wavering will do us no good. Whether one chooses to romanticize or vilify, be primitive man a noble savage or brutish beast, the fact remains that much that was good, much that held traditional societies together is gone now and gone forever. The Haida no longer take Salish slaves, but on the other hand their awe of the forest has been supplanted by a cut-and-run mentality. The practice of killing all comers has evaporated, but on the other hand the village, its generosity and warmth, has gone along with it, too.

I do not pine for a different place and time. I only point out what we have traded off. I think certain good things are re-coverable, though without the life that once surrounded them they must inevitably take on different meanings. One of these is the tradition of parental and communal responsibility for the daily instruction of the young. Today this is denied us because

teaching has been institutionalized, a convenience in a time of
industry and profit when citizen-laborers perform economic
functions more efficiently without children present. But for
whom is such a state of affairs indeed convenient? For the man
or woman who feels lost, unwhole, convenience is beside the
point.

Progressives in the political arena, doing daily battle to re-
humanize capitalism, have given us shorter work days, medical
insurance, maternity leave, and child care. Progressives have
made it steadily more convenient for ordinary people to perform
their economic functions without children getting in the way.
In the long run, though, we have paid the price of cutting our
children loose from the steady moorings of family and community. The children suffer a loss of connectedness, a detach-
ment from the web of communal affairs, a distance from the
life and work of the tribe—and at least as important, we miss
them, too, for similar reasons. Our instinct to nurture through
passing down what we know is blunted because our children
are elsewhere, and besides, what we know is too strange and
esoteric. Most parents feel fondness for those rare, odd moments
when they have knelt close beside a son or daughter to transmit
the mystery of some ancient, incidental craft: tying a bowline,
weaving a pigtail, nipping the suckers from a tomato plant.
These are now Hallmark, quality-time moments, exploited by
advertisers and available on weekends—we want more of them,
we long for that sort of warm proximity in which what we do
is necessary, unforced, and precisely as it should be. In fact, we
move from needing proximity to our parents—feeling the movements of their hands over ours, the warm exhaling of their breath
as they work—to needing proximity to our children. Scott Russell Sanders describes this eloquently in his bittersweet essay
"Reasons of the Body":

I am conscious of my father's example whenever I teach a game to my son. Demonstrating a stroke in tennis or golf, I amplify my gestures, like a ham actor playing to the balcony. My pleasure in the part is increased by the knowledge that others, and especially my father, have played it before me. What I know about hitting a curve or shooting a hook shot or throwing a left jab, I know less by words than by feel. When I take Jesse's hand and curl his fingers over the baseball's red stitches, explaining how to make it deviously spin, I feel my father's hands slip over mine like gloves. Move like so, like so. I feel the same ghostly guidance when I hammer nails or fix a faucet or pluck a banjo. Working on the house or garden or car, I find myself wearing more than my father's hands, find myself clad entirely in his skin.

Sanders acknowledges that "the lore of sports may be all that some fathers have to pass down to their sons in place of lore about hunting animals, planting seeds, killing enemies, or placating the gods." It is unfortunate, even tragic, that this is so, for sport, as Sanders writes, "is a step down from nature": A father's demonstration of a basketball jump shot, while satisfying to both himself and his son, can never replace the day-to-day intimacy fathers and sons shared prior to modernity.

In the end there are reasons beyond education (Can we really detach education from everything else?) to homeschool—a misnomer, in this context, for doing what human beings have always done in bringing up their children. There is a love to be cultivated, an instinct to be nurtured, a need to be satisfied at both ends. Bly writes that "if the son does not actually see what his father does during the day and through all the seasons of the year, a hole will appear in the son's psyche, and the hole will fill with demons who tell him that his father's work is evil and that the father is evil."

But the "hole" appears, it seems to me, in the father's psyche as well. If he cannot share who he is and what he does with the child with whom he feels driven to share it, the hole might grow in him rapidly. The hole begins growing when the father leaves home for work, becomes a chasm opening under him when his child leaves home for school. At this point not only is he exhausted by his labors, he also finds his child is no longer there in the sense he might once have expected. Across the yawning gulf of the dining-room table sits a relative stranger who at thirteen cannot describe for his friends what it is his father does in the world. "He works for Boeing." "He works for IBM." "He works for an insurance company." The details are of course uninteresting, and besides, his friends don't really care.

I grew up in such a home as this, where my father, a good man, was away much. He awoke before dawn and arrived home after dark to read the paper before going to bed. He denied no request to play ball with us; on a few occasions we cleaned the garage side by side, made a trip to the city dump, or washed the car. He drove us to Sunday school, made our lunch afterward, attended our Little League games. In the crowd of fathers huddled on the bleachers he did not stand out particularly—neither yelled nor cursed, on occasion shook his head, made few comments in the game's aftermath. He was foremost a man of philosophical dimensions, cut from an ethical and a gentle cloth, and every day I felt the sheer lack of him. There was a space where my father should have been, a physical space, a void so obvious I didn't grasp it until later, and it explains for me why I enjoyed the Boy Scouts and befriended boys who could teach me about automobile engines and the mysteries of fishing for cutthroat trout. It explains for me, too, the blood hatred for authority I felt at sixteen, a fierce, violent, and all-consuming emotion that centered on my sense of physical superiority (faster, more supple, more dangerous, more *focused*) to my middle-aged high-school teachers. They were the men sent in lieu of my father, and at best they were paltry substitutes. My anger was directed at them for being negligible but also at my father for being absent.

A homeschooling father stays close instead—as close as he can, that is, for in most cases he must work, too, in a world where his children cannot often follow. He wants what was lost to modernity, at least insofar as his children are concerned, though he had better appreciate modernity, too, or go blind with the stars in his eyes. He is selfish in the sense that he grasps for satisfaction by seeking proximity to his children, by venting his need to teach in their direction, and by seeking out a closeness to their sweet scent of play and to their perplexity over, say, a long-division problem. Last weekend, for example, I dug geoducks with my children, a fortuitous pursuit for us all. I took the opportunity to point out while working—as fathers in this part of the world have for thousands of years—that the geoduck doesn't travel but instead retracts its neck, that the point is to dig carefully and to quell one's eagerness, that the shell is fragile, the neck easily slashed, that the butterclams we have broken while digging in the sand will be eaten by sea gulls, that nothing is wasted. A crowd of neighbor children gathered to help, and they too took joy in being there, in the presence of a grown man with specific knowledge about something as tangible as a large clam, and I took joy from their joy. We marveled together as—*swoosh!*—the thing came forth into the sunlight, and when I had finished washing it in the surf a crowd of little heads bent to it silently. I showed them with care what to look for next time—two siphons side by side in the sand, the lips pearly white when compared to a horse clam's, which are dark and coarse, calloused looking. We filled in our holes together. At home again we gathered at the kitchen sink for what a chapter in a home-schooling manual might describe as an anatomy lesson—we pondered the clam's stomach, the long skin that sheathed its neck, the glistening mucus its breast lay in—and again I took pleasure from their pleasure in the moment, so that for me it was more than preparing geoduck to eat. The circle of learning, a kind of womb, enclosed everything else.

It seems to me that all parents must have these moments but that many do not have them often enough to gain sustenance from what they offer. Many are so starved in this regard that they have quit looking to their children for emotional food and have begun to search for it inwardly. The result for some is a dislike of their children on an order and of a scale that befuddles their instincts and that inevitably produces the kind of guilt that yields obligatory—and stale—"quality time." How often have I heard parents demean their children because they are angry about starving at their hands: "I'd better get home before the rug rats get off the bus." "I'm dumping my brats over at Jill's this afternoon so that I can get some shopping done." All these parents want is their daily bread, which they cannot get because, as it turns out, they don't know what it smells like anymore. There are, of course, many reasons for this, but at least one of them is school.

In fact, "I can't wait for school to start again because the kids have been driving me crazy all summer!" is a common complaint in this country. We have even made advertisements out of it: the harried mother who at last gets them out the door with their lunches, books, and rubber rain slickers, then settles into her exotic coffee or a bubble bath and romance novel. What is she doing but feeding herself with food she does not get from her children—food that cannot stick to her bones any more than bath water does? If things go far enough she will gradually learn to treat herself as the neediest child in the house, buying herself toys and then playing with them in various corners of the known universe (men are more prone to this than women): windsurfing here, parasailing there, snorkeling in the tropics while the children attend summer camp, relaxed and at peace when the children are not around, fretful and irritated when they return. She has not learned how to take sustenance from them, is riven by doubts about herself as a mother, cannot understand why she prefers their absence, feels relief when they head for the school bus. The seven-hour respite school provides is in reality a hole she cannot climb from.

Women today, our magazines report, are more exhausted than ever. The reasons for this, while complex and subtle, are also grounded in history. As C. N. Degler points out in *At Odds: Women and the Family in America From the Revolution to the Present*, "The rearing of children and the maintenance of the home had never been a full-time job" prior to the nineteenth century. Today it is often one of two full-time jobs a woman performs without the help of the traditional extended family (an antidote not only for loneliness and hard work but for the intense, obsessive quality, the inward-looking and neurotic tenor, of modern nuclear family life) and often with little help from her husband. In other words, despite the conveniences of modernity she toils longer hours than ever before, and in such a condition her children may come to seem to her like the heaviest part of her burden. School, seen in this light, is a mother's godsend.

Jean Liedloff's important book, *The Continuum Concept*, sheds further light on the plight of modern women, who have been victimized, she says, by child-rearing methods that produce difficult babies. "It is understandable," explains Liedloff, "that Western babies are not welcome in offices, shops, workrooms, or even dinner parties. They usually shriek or kick, wave their arms and stiffen their bodies, so that one needs two hands, and a lot of attention, to keep them under control." Liedloff suggests that more traditional child-rearing patterns—like those of the South American Yequana people she studied and lived among—are sure to produce not only happier babies but happier mothers. "By treating babies the way we did for hundreds of thousands of years," she tells us, "we can be assured of calm, soft, undemanding little creatures. Only then can working mothers, unwilling to be bored and isolated all day with no adult companionship, rid themselves of their cruel conflict. Babies taken to work are where they need to be—with their mothers; and the mothers are where they need to be—with their peers, not doing baby care but something worthy of intelligent adults."

We may find Liedloff's description of happy natives too romantic to be believable. On the other hand, her jungle pastoral is less at issue for us than is the plight of modern women. Caught in the cruel conflict posed by contemporary life, forced to choose between work and children—a choice "primitive" people never confronted—a lot of modern women learn to starve themselves in the name, quite simply, of going on.

Men have not fared much better. Men were long ago extracted from their homes to work in factories, offices, and salt mines. Like women they have suffered at the hands of modernity, and like women they need meaningful relationships with their children if they are to take satisfaction from their lives.

So bringing the children back means bringing ourselves back—we who have been at odds with ourselves for so long now, and so thoroughly. Furthermore, it creates once again in each community the opportunity for the elderly to return to the 'old—grandparents whose lives characteristically lack meaning because they pass with no proximity to the young, whom they need for sustenance as well. You can see them playing golf or raveling in motor homes, too often looking sorrowful. Golf, it should be said, is a good enough game, no more pernicious than any other, and travel as we all know is broadening, and yet it is clear in the eyes of many older people how pointlessly they are grasping at the thin shadow of their former weekend lives. This, sadly, is how they have learned to live in a world that offers them no better place. How natural and right they come to look whenever and wherever their grandchildren are returned to them: Their dignity resurfaces and their confidence of manner; even the words they speak seem more true. They are, of course, the natural teachers that state-certified professionals are meant to replace. But what a paltry substitute I am teaching *Lear* for the grandfather who has come to grasp Lear's dilemma in a way that I cannot. And as much as the children need to hear it from his lips, he needs also to tell it to them.

In many tribal cultures the elders acted first and foremost as teachers. Parents taught too, of course, but more often by going about their tasks while children accompanied them; they explained now and then but mostly demonstrated. Elders, on the other hand, taught consciously, formally, often in the abstract, presenting young people with tales, legends, spiritual wisdom, codes of behavior, principles for living, moral arguments, cosmology, metaphysics, and ethics. It goes without saying that the tribe gained from this its very life and its continuity. Another important outcome, however, was that a person retained a vital role among others far into old age. A man of the coast Salish people could look forward to the day when, though his back might be too bent for the work of canoe building, he would nevertheless be needed by children. He might find among his grandsons one in particular who was as eager to make use of the cedar tree as some children today are to sit before computers, and this boy he would take into the forest. The two of them would sit in the cedar's shelter when it rained so its protective quality became self-evident, and the boy would hear that the cedar had a spirit, that its uses, furthermore, were myriad: boxes, beams, clothes, baskets, mats, hats, canoes. Then the old man would explain what to look for in the cedar's bark, top, and branches and tell the boy how to bring one down without cracking it against the earth. How to move it through the forest, how to build the tools required to work its wood, how to keep the spirit in the tree alive while he turned it into a canoe. The old man would watch while the boy sweated. He would show the boy how to use his palms to gauge hull thickness, how to plane in the canoe's steady rocker, how to steam wide the beam before placing the thwarts, how to scorch in the finish work, how to carve the high prow. The old man's lessons were both practical and spiritual, immediately useful and—just as important—instructions in the right way to live. While the pile of cedar shavings, fragrant and clean, grew on every side of the canoe—the boy squatting in it with his hand adze, working— the old man told stories, reminisced, corrected, remembered aloud his own grandfather. In short he had something to do besides "retiring," something far more satisfying and right: "homeschooling" his grandchild.

Today the accumulated wisdom of our culture is disseminated to the young in classrooms. Front and center, chalk in hand, stands a stranger generally somewhere between twenty-five and fifty-five, full of information arranged into tidy units, none of which seem connected to the others. The young sit while this stranger talks; afterward they move their pens across paper because the stranger says they must. Meanwhile, across town, the elderly have been gathered up in an institution all their own, for like the young they are now in the way of things. Or having labored away from family for forty-five years, having forgotten how to find their satisfaction there, they go off in search of it in motor homes and golf carts. How much more we offer ourselves, and them, by asking our elderly to help educate our children. Our world is more volatile, less changeless, than the Salish world, so certainly there is much our elderly can't teach. Still, we need desperately what they *can* give before our best traditions are lost to us.

Again, we do ourselves no good by romanticizing tribal peoples, but we do ourselves no good dismissing them either. We can glean from their lives much that holds the promise to improve our own—their feeling for the earth they inhabited is the most obvious example. Perhaps, too, we might objectively contemplate their manner of educating their young and, while recognizing that our world is not theirs, that much has changed, find not only ways that work for children but—at least as important—a way toward greater meaning for ourselves.

For thousands of years, in thousands of places, families educated their own. This tradition changed not because a better method was found but because economic conditions required it. To work one had to leave one's children; one's children, furthermore, had to be trained for tasks no one in their purview could be seen doing. For these reasons institutionalized schooling was invented, and while it adequately addressed a set of economic problems it inspired a new set of human ones that are psychological, emotional, and even spiritual in nature. This latter set of problems still haunts us, and many now want to come to terms with it. Some have found that the solution is to homeschool, and while they do so chiefly because it works extraordinarily well, providing both academically and socially for their children's needs, they also do it because it fulfills their own desire, an instinctive and undeniable one. To give their children over to an institution is to deny themselves certain elemental satisfactions that life as a parent has to offer. They know this, are reluctant and ultimately unwilling to give up these fulfillments, and this as much as anything explains why they teach their own.

It would be an act of extraordinary selfishness if the children didn't also benefit. And there is always the danger that parental desire of this sort might overwhelm children when it operates outside the tribal context. Nonindustrial people always had one another; their children learned from everybody. But to home-school in the contemporary world means something else altogether. A traditional undertaking in a modern context, it is potentially a defensive maneuver, a fending off or entrenching tactic, a commitment made out of fear, not love, and thus dangerous to the child's—and our nation's—well-being. In the end it cannot be done well without a love that looks beyond the closed world of the nuclear family. It can't be done well without the larger love of a community—and nation—that takes teaching and learning to heart.

Notes on Sources

Introduction

5 Pinpointing the number of homeschoolers in the United States is a problematic task. Patricia Lines, a senior research associate in the Office of Educational Research and Improvement, United States Department of Education, is widely considered the foremost authority on this subject. Lines' article, "Home Instruction: The Size and Growth of the Movement," in Jane Van Galen and Mary Anne Pittman, eds., *Home Schooling: Political, Historical, and Pedagogical Perspectives* (Norwood, N.J.: Ablex Publishing Corporation, 1991), is a clear account of her method in arriving at a useful estimate. Based on data gathered through 1989, Lines estimates the number of American homeschoolers at between two hundred thousand and three hundred thousand. Her more recent paper, "Estimating the Home Schooled Population" (U.S. Dept. of Education, Office of Research, Washington, D.C., 20208), puts the number at between two hundred fifty and three hundred fifty thousand for the 1990–91 school year. If the number has continued to grow at the implied rate, then the 1992 figure is upward of three hundred thousand, perhaps as high as half a million, as Sam Allis reported in the October 22, 1990, issue of *Time*.

5 Lists of famous homeschoolers pose a sticky problem. Do those professionally tutored at home qualify as homeschoolers? What about those who attended school for a time before dropping out?

Do we think of those who received their educations prior to the advent of schools—such as George Washington—as home-schoolers? A helpful source is Malcolm Plent's pamphlet "Famous Homeschoolers" (Unschooling Network, 2 South Street, Farmingdale, N.J., 07727, 1986), which includes entries on Woodrow Wilson, Thomas Edison, and Noël Coward.

7 *The Christian Educator* is a newsletter published by Christian Liberty Academy, a correspondence school located in Arlington Heights, Illinois. I have quoted from an editorial by P. Lindstrom that appeared on page 2 of the December 1985 issue.

Teacher, Parent

11 Criticisms of standardized tests are by now ubiquitous. However, the National Commission on Testing and Public Policy's *From Gatekeeper to Gateway: Transforming Testing in America* (Chestnut Hill, Mass.: National Commission on Testing and Public Policy, Boston College, 1990) is singularly authoritative.

11 My information on homeschoolers and standardized tests derives chiefly from two sources. The first is Dr. Brian D. Ray's *Home School Researcher*, a publication of the National Home Education Research Institute (Western Baptist College, 5000 Deer Park Dr. SE, Salem, Oreg., 97301). Ray provides a useful summary of homeschooling research in "Home Schools: A Synthesis of Research on Characteristics and Learner Outcomes," which originally appeared in *Education and Urban Society*, Vol. 21, No. 1, November 1988, pages 16–31. My other vital source was a series of reports compiled by the Washington Homeschool Research Project (16109 Northeast 169 Place, Woodinville, Wash. 98072), spearheaded by public school counselor Jon Wartes. See also Hank Whittemore's article "The Most Precious Gift" (*Parade* magazine, December 22, 1991, page 4) for the extraordinary story of Robert Howard Allen, who graduated summa cum laude from Bethel College without any prior formal schooling.

12 For an excellent discussion of coaching and the SAT see David Owens's *None of the Above: Behind the Myth of Scholastic Aptitude* (Boston: Houghton Mifflin, 1985). The Educational Testing Service discusses coaching in *10 SATs* (New York: College Entrance Examination Board, 1983).

15 I am indebted to Patrick Farenga's article "Homeschoolers and College," which appears in *Schooling at Home: Parents, Kids and Learning* (Anne Pedersen and Peggy O'Mara, eds., Santa Fe: John Muir, 1990), for information on homeschoolers who have gone on to successful college careers.

16 Bennett underscores the crucial educative role of parents on page 20 of *Our Children and Our Country* (New York: Touchstone, 1989); Bloom discusses family life and education on pages 57–58 of *The Closing of the American Mind* (New York: Touchstone, 1987).

17 Hirsch is quoted from page 114 of *Cultural Literacy: What Every American Needs to Know* (New York: Vintage, 1988). His critique of the Coleman Report appears on pages 113–16.

17 The work of James S. Coleman has been widely discussed and written about. Coleman's study appears in *Equality of Educational Opportunity* (Washington, D.C.: Government Printing Office, 1966). The essential companion piece, it seems to me, is C. Jencks, et al., *Inequality: A Reassessment of the Effect of Family and Schooling in America* (New York: Basic Books, 1972).

18 The *Newsweek*-commissioned poll I refer to—"The PTA/Dodge National Parent Survey"—is available from The National PTA, 700 Rush Street, Chicago, Ill., 60611-2571.

18 For more on James P. Comer's New Haven studies see his *School Power: Implications of an Intervention Project* (New York: Macmillan Publishing Co., 1980).

18–19 Figures on suicide rates are from page 137 of Merry White's *The Japanese Educational Challenge: A Commitment to*

Children (New York: The Free Press, 1987); the quote is from page 14. White's book is a forceful account of the role family plays in Japan's educational success.

21 Mrs. Zajac is the heroine of Tracy Kidder's *Among Schoolchildren* (New York: Avon, 1989).

24 Farenga discusses mastery learning in "Methodologies and Curricula," an article appearing in *Schooling at Home: Parents, Kids, and Learning* (see note 15).

26 John Holt's essential work is *Teach Your Own* (New York: Delacorte Press, 1981). The reference to freedom in education is from pages 168–69.

What About Democracy?

40 Bill McFadden refers to Jefferson's "Notes on the State of Virginia," which appears in *The Portable Jefferson*, Merrill D. Peterson, ed. (New York: Viking, 1975); and "Bill for the More General Diffusion of Knowledge," from *The Works of Thomas Jefferson*, Vol. II, page 414 (New York: G. P. Putnam and Sons, 1905). He also refers to Washington's 1796 Farewell Address, which appears on page 214 of *The Writings of George Washington* (Washington, D.C.: U.S. Government Printing Office, 1946), and the twelfth of Horace Mann's annual reports on education, from *Life and Works of Horace Mann,* Mary Mann, ed., Vol. 3 (Boston: Horace B. Fuller, 1868).

41 Figures on inequities between school districts come from Ginny Carroll's article "Who Foots the Bill?" in *Newsweek's* September 1990 special issue on education.

42 John Goodlad discusses use of instructional time on page 229 of *A Place Called School* (New York: McGraw-Hill, 1984).

42 Ernest Boyer's conclusions were published in *High School: A Report on Secondary Education in America* (Princeton, N.J.: Carnegie Foundation for the Advancement of Teaching, 1983).

42–43 Walter Karp's trenchant account of school inequality and special privilege, "Why Johnny Can't Think: The Politics of Bad

Schooling," appeared in the June 1985 issue of *Harper's*. See the article "Indochinese Refugee Families and Academic Achievement," by Nathan Caplan, Marcella H. Choy, and John K. Whitemore (*Scientific American*, February 1992, pages 36–42), for more on the Indochinese refugee children. The authors write that their research findings "point overwhelmingly to the pivotal role of the family" in academic success.

45 Dewey wrote about democracy and schools in a number of books, including *The School and Society* (Chicago: University of Chicago Press, 1956) and *Democracy and Education* (New York: MacMillan, 1916).

46 I quote from a speech Hitler delivered on May 1, 1937, excerpted on page 249 of William L. Shirer's *The Rise and Fall of the Third Reich* (New York: Simon and Schuster, 1960).

48 Nina Darnton describes New Orleans's home-instruction program in her article "A Mother's Touch" (*Newsweek* special education issue, September 1990).

Homeschoolers Among Others

54 The Taylor and Montgomery studies are available from the National Home Education Research Institute.

55 The 1986 Washington State survey is from the Washington Homeschool Research Project (see second note 11).

56 An excellent discussion of the tracking issue is *Keeping Track: How Schools Structure Inequality*, by Jennie Oakes (New Haven: Yale University Press, 1985). For further insight into socialization and the schools see Penelope Eckert's *Jocks and Burnouts: Social Categories and Identity in the High School* (New York: Teachers College Press, 1989).

60 I quote Dewey from *The School and Society* (see note 45), pages 43–44.

67 The activities of homeschoolers beyond their homes are often described in the excellent bimonthly newsletter *Growing Without Schooling*, available from the organization of the same name, 2269 Massachusetts Avenue, Cambridge, Mass. 02140. Britt

Barker describes her experiences in *Letters Home* (1990), available from Home Education Press, P. O. Box 1083, Tonasket, Wash. 98855.

My Father Comes to Class

78 There are two comprehensive guides to homeschooling legal matters. The first is *Home Education and Constitutional Liberties*, by John W. Whitehead and Wendell R. Bird (Westchester, Ill.: Crossway Books, 1984); the second is *Home Schooling and the Law*, by Michael P. Farris (Paeonian Springs, Va: Home School Legal Defense Association, 1990). Most references in this chapter derive from these two sources.

Stephen Arons' book *Compelling Belief: The Culture of American Schooling* (New York: McGraw Hill, 1983) is a helpful and in-depth discussion of a few individual cases. John Holt has also written on legal matters, particularly in *Teach Your Own* (see note 26). Articles by Perry Zirkel, in the *Phi Delta Kappan* and elsewhere, provide a counterbalance to the aforementioned writers, all of whom refer mostly to cases favorable to homeschoolers. Zirkel is more apt to discuss cases that have gone both ways.

School, Home, and History

101 The Mbuti people are discussed in Colin M. Turnbull's *The Human Cycle* (New York: Simon and Schuster, 1983). Mead—a homeschooler herself—discusses empathetic and imitative learning in Chapter 4 of *Continuities in Cultural Evolution* (New Haven: Yale University Press, 1964).

102–3 My information on Egyptian and German Pietist schools comes from a basic and vital source: *The Encyclopaedia Britannica,* which includes an excellent ninety-one page article on the history of education.

103 *The Emile of Jean Jacques Rousseau, Selections,* is translated and edited by William Boyd (New York: Bureau of Publication, Teachers College, Columbia University, 1956).

104–5 The Latin Schools and our early academies are discussed in *Education in a Free Society: An American History,* by S. Alexander Rippa (White Plains, N.Y.: Longman Inc., 1967).

105 John Taylor Gatto, in his 1990 New York City Teacher of the Year Award acceptance speech (reprinted in the September/October 1990 *Utne Reader*), referred to a paper released by Senator Ted Kennedy's office claiming a 98 percent literacy rate in Massachusetts prior to compulsory schooling. La Rouchefault Liancourt, in *Travels Through the United States of North America* (London, 1799), observes that "hardly a person can be met with in Connecticut, any more than in Massachusetts, who is not qualified to read, write and perform the common operations of arithmetic." Kenneth Lockeridge, in *Literacy in Colonial New England* (New York: Norton, 1974), notes on page 4 that New England achieved "nearly universal male literacy toward the end of the colonial period," long before the advent of compulsory schooling. Further, the well-known historian Lawrence Cremins notes on page 546 of *American Education: The Colonial Experience 1607–1783* (New York: Harper & Row, 1970) that "adult male literacy in the American colonies seems to have run from 70 per cent to virtually 100 per cent." Also of interest is this passage from page 550 of Cremins:

> Of the fifty-six signers of the Declaration, twenty-two were products of the provincial colleges, two had attended the academy conducted by Francis Allen at New London, Pennsylvania, and the others represented every conceivable combination of parental, church, apprenticeship, school, tutorial and self-education, including some who had studied abroad. Of the thirty-three signers of the Constitution who had not also signed the Declaration, fourteen were products of the provincial colleges, one was a product of the Newark academy, and the remainder spanned the same range of alternative patterns.

Finally, William J. Gilmore, on page 116 of *Reading Becomes a Necessity of Life: Material and Cultural Life in Rural New England 1780–1835* (Knoxville: The University of Tennessee Press, 1989), observes that "by 1800 in rural northwestern New England the overwhelming majority of both male and female adults, untouched by the process of urbanization underway to the south, had learned to read and write in their childhood or youth." All of this should be compared to the oft-cited statistic of about 50 percent functional illiteracy in America at the end of the twentieth century.

106 The quote is from pages 16–17 of Colin Greer's *The Great School Legend* (New York: Basic Books, 1972).

106 Michael B. Katz, an important revisionist historian, challenges the standard view of American educational history in *Reconstructing American Education* (Cambridge, Mass.: Harvard University Press, 1987). Katz's *The Irony of Early School Reform: Educational Innovation in Mid-Nineteenth Century Massachusetts* (Boston: Beacon, 1968) is also important reading. Perhaps the most influential revisionist work, though, is *Schooling in Capitalist America*, by Samuel Bowles and Herbert Gintis (New York: Basic Books, 1976). The revisionists are ably critiqued by Diane Ravitch in *The Revisionists Revisited: A Critique of the Radical Attack on the Schools* (New York: Basic Books, 1978).

107 Rippa (see note 104–5) discusses Mann's clashes with forces opposed to the common schools on pages 101–7. For more on the growth of the common schools see Charles Glenn's excellent *The Myth of the Common School* (Amherst, Mass.: The University of Massachusetts Press, 1987).

107 The incident in Barnstable is referred to by John Taylor Gatto in his New York City Teacher of the Year acceptance speech (see note 105). Katz (see second note 106) also discusses recalcitrant Barnstable parents on page 46.

107 Joseph Kirschner's article "The Shifting Role of Family and School as Educator: A Historical Perspective," which appears in *Home Schooling: Political, Historical, and Pedagogical Perspectives* (see first note 5), illuminates those forces that undermined the family's educative role in the nineteenth century.

108 Katz discusses events in Beverly on pages 20–21 of *The Irony of*

Early School Reform (see second note 106). Rippa (see note 104–5) discusses the *Kalamazoo* decision on page 116.

110 Dewey's Laboratory School is discussed on pages 135–42 of Lawrence Cremin's *The Transformation of the School: Progressivism in American Education, 1876–1957* (New York: Vintage, 1961).

112–13 The passage on open schools is from pages 68–69 of *Doing Your Own School*, by the Great Atlantic and Pacific School Conspiracy (Boston: Beacon, 1972). The reference to the East Harlem Block School is from page 81.

113 For more from the sixties read George Dennison's *The Lives of Children* (New York: Random House, 1969), Jonathan Kozol's *Death at an Early Age* (New York: Houghton Mifflin, 1967), Herbert Kohl's *The Open Classroom* (New York: Vintage, 1969), John Holt's *How Children Learn* (New York: Pitman, 1967), and James Herndon's *The Way It Spozed to Be* (New York: Simon and Schuster, 1968).

Abiding Questions

119 Plato describes his ideas regarding education in *The Republic*, translated by B. Jowett (New York: Modern Library, 1941). Jowett also translated Aristotle's *Politics* (New York: Colonial Press, 1899).

121 John Taylor Gatto refers to Bertrand Russell and the dialectic in his speech "The Congregational Principle," which like the other Gatto speeches mentioned here is available in text by writing Gatto at 235 West 76th Street, New York, N.Y., 10023.

122 Alfred North Whitehead's comment on Plato is from Part I, Chapter 1, Section 3, of *Process and Reality* (New York: Free Press, 1979).

124 Dewey's comments on Rousseau are from page 61 of *Schools of Tomorrow* (New York: Dutton, 1915), co-authored by Evelyn Dewey. In general Dewey is difficult to follow. Try *The School*

and Society and *Democracy and Education* (see note 45) for relatively clear accounts of his ideas.

126 Illich is quoted from pages 49 and 15, respectively, of *Deschooling Society* (New York: Harper & Row, 1970). For a useful discussion of Illich's thought see *After Deschooling, What?*, Alan Gartner, Colin Greer, and Frank Riesman, eds. (New York: Perennial Library, 1973).

127 Holt's affirmation of Illich appears on page 189 of *Freedom and Beyond* (New York: Delta, 1972).

128 Dewey is quoted from page 7 of *The School and Society* (see note 45).

128 Susan Douglas Fransoza criticizes Holt's thought in her article "The Best and Wisest Parent: A Critique of John Holt's Philosophy of Education," which appears on page 123 of *Home Schooling: Political, Historical, and Pedagogical Perspectives* (see first note 5).

The Matter of Money

132 The 85 percent figure is conservative. *Newsweek's* September 1990 special education issue cites a Bureau of Labor Statistics report that only 7 percent of school-age children now live in two-parent households where there is only one wage earner.

132–33 Mary Wendy Roberts, commissioner of the Oregon Bureau of Labor and Industries, is quoted from her column in the *New York Times* on August 30, 1991.

137 Information on Washington State's education budget is from *Financing Public Schools in Washington State*, prepared by the Olympia Educational Service District No. 114, September 1990.

137 Gatto is quoted from his speech "Why Do Bad Schools Cost So Much?" (see note 121). For his statistics regarding funding in New York's schools Gatto credits a paper ("Choice, Funding, and Pupil Achievement," by Bruce S. Cooper, Robert Sarrel, and Toby Tetenbaum, Fordham University) given on April 18, 1990, at the American Education Research Association's Annual Meeting.

139 The Kansas City schools are briefly discussed in the article " 'Choice' Plans Should Include Private Option," by John E. Coons, *Education Week,* January 17, 1990.

140 James B. Hunt, Jr., discusses the interest and involvement of business leaders in education in "Education for Economic Growth: A Critical Investment," *Phi Delta Kappan,* April 1984. The quote is from page 5 of David T. Kearns and Denis P. Doyle's *Winning the Brain Race: A Bold Plan to Make Our Schools Competitive* (San Francisco: ICS Press, 1989).

141 Frank Shrontz discusses business and education in his article "Can America Compete?" which appears on the January 19, 1992, editorial page of the *Seattle Times.*

141 This excerpt from *A Nation at Risk: The Imperative for Educational Reform* (Washington, D.C.: U.S. Government Printing Office, 1983) can be found on page 5.

141 Joel Spring discusses the post–World War II history of business's influence on the schools in "Education and the Sony Way," *Phi Delta Kappan,* April 1984.

143 I quote from page 5 of *A Nation at Risk* (see second note 141).

143 For more on school-year length read Michael S. Barrett's article "The Case for More School Days," in the *Atlantic,* November 1990.

145–46 I've excerpted Gatto from a speech he delivered November 2, 1990, at the Hotel Inter-Continental, New York City, called "We Can't Afford School Reform" (see note 121).

147 "Hot for School" appeared in the Wednesday, August 14, 1991, *Seattle Times.*

147–48 These Texas Instruments and Amway advertisements appeared in *Newsweek*'s September 1990 issue on education.

150 Data on the average annual income of homeschooling families were compiled from a number of sources cited by Ray in "Home Schools: A Synthesis of Research on Characteristics and Learner Outcomes" (see second note 11).

Before Schools

155 Erik Erikson is quoted from page 143 of *Childhood and Society* (New York: Norton, 1950).

156–57 Mead describes the Cheyenne children on page 64 of *Continuities in Cultural Evolution* (see note 101).

157 Honigmann discusses education among the Kaskan people on page 185 of "Culture and Ethos of Kaska Society," an article appearing in *Yale University Publications in Anthropology*, Vol. 40 (New Haven: Yale University Press, 1949). Romantics should read Honigmann thoroughly: Many details of Kaskan life, especially those regarding warfare, are not readily romanticized.

159–60 References to the educational methods of nonindustrial peoples in this chapter are mostly from the Human Relations Area File (HRAF to librarians), a standard source in microfiche for anthropological data. Particularly useful are entries under the headings "Educational Theories and Methods" and "Transmission of Beliefs." The material about the Nupe is from Siegfried Nadel's *The King's Hangmen*; the quote about the Seminoles is from Charles Fairbanks' *The Florida Seminole People*. The reference to the Trukese is from Frank Joseph Mahoney's *A Trukese Theory of Medicine*. Hilger is cited from *A Social Study of 150 Chippewa Indian Families*. All appear in HRAF.

161 Ray Kroc never finished high school. He tells his story in *Grinding It Out: The Making of McDonald's* (New York: Saint Martin's Press, 1977).

162 Resnick's 1987 Presidential Address to the AERA entitled "Learning in School and Out," was reprinted in the December 1987 issue of the *Educational Researcher*.

163 Twain's advice is often repeated and is at the same time perhaps apocryphal, a part of American folklore.

163 Frost is quoted from page 412 of *Robert Frost: Poetry and Prose*, E. C. Lathem and L. Thompson, eds. (New York: Henry Holt, 1972).

166–67 I am deeply indebted in this portion of the chapter to Robert LeVine and Merry White's excellent *Human Conditions: The Cultural Basis of Educational Development* (New York: Routledge & Kegan Paul, 1986). The two quotes are, in order, from pages 194 and 212.

What We've Learned About How We Learn

171 Jerome Bruner's books include *The Process of Education* (New York: Vintage Books, Random House, 1960), *Toward a Theory of Instruction* (Cambridge: Harvard University Press, 1966), and *In Search of Mind: Essays in Autobiography* (New York: Harper and Row, 1983).

172 Sylvia Farnham-Diggory is cited from pages 49 and 50 of her book *Schooling* (Cambridge: Harvard University Press, 1990).

173–74 Harper Lee's *To Kill a Mockingbird* (New York: Lippincott, 1960) is especially interesting to read with the subject of homeschooling in mind.

174 David Ausubel discusses his ideas in *Educational Psychology: A Cognitive View* (New York: Holt, Rinehart and Winston, 1968) and "The Use of Advance Organizers in the Learning and Retention of Meaningful Verbal Material," *Journal of Educational Psychology*, Vol. 51, 1960, pages 267–72. Joseph D. Novak illuminates Ausubel's thought in *A Theory of Education* (Ithaca, N.Y.: Cornell University Press, 1977).

176 Terry Borton's book is *Reach, Touch and Teach: Student Concerns and Process Education* (New York: McGraw-Hill, 1970). William Watson Purkey's book is *Self Concept and School Achievement* (Englewood Cliffs, N.J.: Prentice-Hall, 1970).

177–80 Howard Gardner makes the case for varying intelligences in *Frames of Mind: The Theory of Multiple Intelligences* (New York: Basic Books, 1983). The quote on autonomous intelligences is from page 8; the quote on early identification of them from page 10. Gardner discusses the difficulty of defining distinct intelligences in Chapter 4, pages 59–70; he reminds social planners of their duty to "the wider society" on page 392.

Many writers have taken up Gardner's ideas, foremost among them Thomas Armstrong in *In Their Own Way: Discovering and Encouraging Your Child's Personal Learning Style* (Los Angeles, Jeremy P. Tarcher, 1987).

Schools and Families: A Proposal

186 Twin Ridges' home-study program is described in "Home Study and the Public Schools," by Geeta Dardick, in *Schooling at Home: Parents, Kids, and Learning* (see note 15). Dardick's daughter, Samantha, was enrolled in Twin Ridges' program.

187 Twin Ridges' *Home Study Newsletter* lists as its address P. O. Box 529, North San Juan, Calif. 95960.

189 For more on legal requirements in Washington see *Washington State's Laws Regulating Home-Based Instruction*, available from the Superintendent of Public Instruction, Old Capitol Building, FG-11, Olympia, Wash. 98504-3211.

190 The Seneca Valley School District's Administrative Center is at 725 West New Castle Street, Zelienople, Pa. 16063-1027.

193 The Lake Washington School District is at 6500 111th Avenue NE, Kirkland, Wash. 98033.

A Life's Work

217 Sanders is quoted from page 211 of his book *Secrets of the Universe: Scenes from the Journey Home* (Boston: Beacon Press, 1991).

217–18 In this passage from page 21 of *Iron John* (Reading, Mass.: Addison-Wesley, 1990), Bly credits the German psychologist Alexander Mitscherlich with having formulated the "hole" image. Mitscherlich's book *Society Without the Father* (London: Tavistock, 1969) makes an interesting accompaniment to Bly.

221 Degler is cited from page 81 of *At Odds: Women and Children*

in America from the Revolution to the Present (Oxford: Oxford University, 1980).

221 Liedloff discusses the plight of modern women on pages x and xi of her introduction to *The Continuum Concept* (Reading, Mass.: Addison-Wesley, 1977).

Further Reading

There are few good books available on homeschooling. I like David and Micki Colfax's *Homeschooling for Excellence* (New York: Warner Books, 1988). The Colfaxes have homeschooled four children—the youngest two adopted—three of whom have been successful students at Harvard (the fourth is not yet college age). Also useful is Howard and Susan Richman's *The Three R's at Home* (Kittanning, Pa.: Pennsylvania Homeschoolers, 1988). Howard Richman later authored *Story of a Bill: Legalizing Homeschooling in Pennsylvania* (Kittanning, Pa.: Pennsylvania Homeschoolers, 1989).

Schooling at Home: Parents, Kids, and Learning (see note 15, page 229) is helpful and contains a list of resources and references for those interested in homeschooling, including curricula, periodicals, homeschooling organizations, and educational-supply catalogs.

How-to homeschooling books are readily available in many libraries. None seem to me as useful as *Growing Without Schooling* (see note 67, page 231), the bimonthly newsletter from the organization of the same name (2269 Massachusetts Avenue, Cambridge, Mass. 02140—[617] 864-3100). Each issue provides lists of helpful resources, a book order catalogue, an exchange of ideas and information between homeschoolers, and news about local homeschooling groups. *GWS* also tracks homeschooling legislation nationwide and reports on legal matters. However, those interested in definitive information about the legality of homeschooling should contact their local school district office or state board of education.

Homeschoolers are a contentious lot. The politics of the movement are often disconcerting. A great variety of leaders and organizations have put themselves forward as representing homeschoolers. Libertarians and progressives war with right-wing Christians; meanwhile politically moderate Christians have become incensed at being "represented" by fundamentalists. Joining a homeschooling organization is akin to choosing sides in a battle. Those interested in a side trip down this alley might take a look at the article "Homeschooling Freedoms at Risk" in the May/June issue of *Home Education Magazine*, P. O. Box 1083, Tonasket, Wash. 98855, with the understanding that it presents only one side of the matter.

Jean Liedloff's *The Continuum Concept*—an unfortunate title for such a thought-provoking book—is essential to those interested in anthropology and education. Liedloff spent two and a half years living among native peoples in South America. Other important works of anthropology are Colin Turnbull's *The Human Cycle* and Edward T. Hall's *Beyond Culture* (New York: Doubleday, 1976). For me the best look at culture and education is White and LeVine's *Human Conditions* (see note 166–67 on page 239).

Popular, readable, and important books on education include Jonathan Kozol's recent *Savage Inequalities* (New York: Crown, 1991) and Tracy Kidder's *Among Schoolchildren* (New York: Avon, 1990). For more on democracy and education see *Choosing Equality: The Case for Democratic Schools*, Ann Bastian, Norm Fruchter, Marilyn Gittell, Colin Greer, and Kenneth Haskins, eds. (Philadelphia: Temple U. Press, 1985); and *Schooling for All: Class, Race and the Decline of the Democratic Ideal*, by Ira Katznelson and Margaret Weir (New York: Basic Books, 1985). Two good histories are Lawrence Cremin's *The Transformation of the School* (New York: Vintage, 1961) and David Tyack's *Turning Points in American Educational History* (Lexington, Mass.: Xerox College Publishing, 1967). Tyack is also the author of *Learning Together: A History of Coeducation in American Schools* (New Haven: Yale University Press, 1990), an excellent book about gender and education.

Joel Spring's *The Sorting Machine Revisited* (New York: Longman, 1988) discusses the schools as agents of control for a corporate state. See also Spring's *The Sorting Machine: National Educational Policy Since 1945* (New York: David McKay, 1976) and *Education and the Rise of the Corporate State* (Boston: Beacon Press, 1972).

There are many good books on American high schools, including Theodore Sizer's *Horace's Compromise: The Dilemma of the American High School* (Boston: Houghton Mifflin, 1984) and Arthur Powell, Eleanor Farrar, and David Cohen's *The Shopping Mall High School: Winners and Losers in the Educational Marketplace* (Boston: Houghton Mifflin, 1985).

Finally, I recommend two works of fiction to anyone pondering schooling at home: Paul Theroux's *The Mosquito Coast* (New York: Avon, 1982) and Jane Smiley's novella "Good Will," which appears in *Ordinary Love and Good Will* (New York: Knopf, 1989).

My thanks go not only to the above authors but to many others who, though they may not have been cited specifically, have contributed much to my thinking about education. I am indebted to every one of them.

Index

Index

Elderly and homeschooling, 222–25
Elitism and homeschooling, 39–40, 47, 128
Emile (Rousseau), 103–5, 124
Erikson, Erik, 155
Everything I Need to Know I Learned in Kindergarten (Fulghum), 4

Family
  educational role of the, 16–19, 27, 43, 49, 63, 106–8, 137, 143–44, 167, 183–204
  effects of industrialization on the, 107, 166, 210–11, 214–26
  influence on academic success, 16–19, 143–44
  as key to educational reform, 183–84, 195, 201, 203
  life, changes in, 132–36, 215–26
  as political catchword, 134
  socioeconomics of the, 107, 132–39, 149–51
  in traditional cultures, 159–60, 166–67
Farnham-Diggory, Sylvia, 172
Farrington v. Tokushige (1927), 85–86, 97
Frames of Mind (Gardner), 180
Franklin, Benjamin, 83, 104–5
Freedom and Beyond (Holt), 127
Froebel, Friedrich, 125
Frost, Robert, 163
Fulghum, Robert, 4, 209

Gardner, Howard, 177–80
Gaskins, Henry, 148
Gatto, John Taylor, 137, 145–46
German Pietist schools, 103

Goodlad, John, 42, 145
Goodman, Paul, 113
Great Atlantic and Pacific School Conspiracy, 112
Group School, The (Cambridge, Massachusetts), 112
Growing Without Schooling, 114
Guarani Indians, 157–58

Haida Indians, 215
Harvard Project on Human Potential, 177
Herndon, James, 113, 176
Hilger, W. Inez, 160
Hinton v. Kentucky Board of Education (1978), 96–97
Hirsch, E. D., Jr., 2, 16–17, 27
Hitler, Adolf, 46
Holt, John, 26, 113–14, 118, 125–29, 176
Homeschooled children. *See also* Homeschooler(s); Homeschooling
  academic success of, 6, 11, 14–16, 114
  vs. schooled children, 11, 14, 54–55, 64–65, 69, 94
  scores of, on standardized achievement tests, 6, 11, 14–16, 20, 92–93, 95, 189
  socialization of, 51–55, 61–65, 67–71
Homeschooler(s). *See also* Homeschooled children; Homeschooling; Homeschooling parents
  defined, 5
  famous, 5, 15, 105
  as misnomer, 5, 64,
  number of, in U.S., 5, 114